GRACE MOMENTS
JULY-SEPTEMBER 2025

TIME OF GRACE

Published by Straight Talk Books
P.O. Box 301, Milwaukee, WI 53201
800.661.3311 / timeofgrace.org

Copyright © 2025 Time of Grace Ministry

All rights reserved. This publication may not be copied, photocopied, reproduced, translated, or converted to any electronic or machine-readable form in whole or in part, except for brief quotations, without prior written approval from Time of Grace Ministry.

Unless otherwise indicated, Scripture is taken from THE HOLY BIBLE, NEW INTERNATIONAL VERSION®, NIV®. Copyright © 1973, 1978, 1984, 2011 by Biblica, Inc.® Used by permission. All rights reserved worldwide.

Scripture marked CSB is taken from The Christian Standard Bible. Copyright © 2017 by Holman Bible Publishers. Used by permission. Christian Standard Bible®, and CSB® are federally registered trademarks of Holman Bible Publishers. All rights reserved.

Scripture marked NLT is taken from the *Holy Bible*, New Living Translation, copyright © 1996, 2004, 2015 by Tyndale House Foundation. Used by permission of Tyndale House Publishers, Inc., Carol Stream, Illinois 60188. All rights reserved.

Printed in the United States of America
ISBN: 978-1-965694-27-5

TIME OF GRACE *is a registered mark of Time of Grace Ministry.*

JULY

Remember your leaders, who spoke the word of God to you. Consider the outcome of their way of life and imitate their faith.

HEBREWS 13:7

July 1

Everyone is spiritual
Mike Novotny

You might think that spirituality in America is in decline, but you would be wrong. Spiritual things are everywhere. He owns a Bible, believes in guardian angels, and speaks of a "higher power." She listens to the pope, prays the rosary, and lights a candle with the image of the virgin Mary. He believes in luck, checks his horoscope, and stops by church when he needs God's help. She calls herself Christian, is curious about Buddhism, but mostly trusts her gut. A few talk of doctrine, dogma, and Christian creeds. Most prefer terms like *spirituality* and *faith journey*. How about you and your friends?

While the mix-and-match approach to faith might be popular, Paul offers a warning about general spirituality: **"You know that when you were pagans, somehow or other you were influenced and led astray to mute idols"** (1 Corinthians 12:2). One of the (many) problems with idols is they are "mute," unable to speak to you. In the end, you are stuck with merely human opinions, mostly your own.

But our God is not mute. **"No one has ever seen God, but the one and only Son, who is himself God and is in closest relationship with the Father, has made him known"** (John 1:18). There are countless reasons that we love being devoutly Christian instead of vaguely spiritual. Near the top is the stability we find in a God who talks, a Jesus who speaks to us of the Father's love.

If you're going to believe in something, believe in the God who speaks clear words of truth and love.

July 2

Never alone
Matt Ewart

Most of the sayings in the book of Proverbs are inspiring or insightful, but this one feels downright depressing: **"Each heart knows its own bitterness, and no one else can share its joy"** (Proverbs 14:10). This proverb reminds you that being human can be lonely. Whether you feel immense joy or crushing sadness, you are the only one who can fully experience what you do.

No matter how well you express your emotions, words never can capture fully the depth of what you feel. No matter how clearly your body language conveys happiness or grief, it can't transfer your emotions into someone else's heart. Being human can be lonely.

But Jesus changed that. When God became human, he didn't just observe your struggles. He lived them. He felt the depths of sorrow, exhaustion, and betrayal. He experienced the loneliness of the human condition so that he could do something about it. His death and resurrection mean you are never truly alone.

Now his Spirit dwells in you by faith. Even when you don't have the words to express what's on your heart, the Spirit intercedes for you **"through wordless groans"** (Romans 8:26). And Jesus, your perfect High Priest, stands before the Father on your behalf, knowing exactly what you need.

Jesus knows. He understands. He walks with you in every moment—rejoicing in your joy, grieving in your sorrow, and carrying you when you feel weak.

You are never alone. Not for a single moment.

July 3

Jesus, this is why you came
Ann Jahns

A few years ago, my oldest brother died unexpectedly. As I watched my mom weeping over her son's body, I thought, *Jesus, this is why you came.*

In the dark days that followed, which were hazy with shock and grief and the necessary practicalities that follow a death, I thought, *Jesus, this is why you came.*

During my brother's funeral as the familiar words of Scripture and his favorite hymns washed over us, reminding us that those who die in Christ will live forever, I thought, *Jesus, this is why you came.*

Jesus willingly came into our mess of a world. Why? He tells us: **"I have come into the world as a light, so that no one who believes in me should stay in darkness"** (John 12:46).

Jesus didn't come to make life easy. Or to have it make sense. Jesus came to shine his light into the darkness of our sin. He came to die in our place, that through his death and resurrection, we can someday worship a holy God forever in a place free from sickness, pain, weeping, and death.

The next time you stand in front of an open casket or an open grave, remember, *Jesus, this is why you came.* In the end, he will make all things right. All will be made new. All will be restored. There will be no more unexpected death, no more funeral arrangements, no more moms burying their sons. *Jesus, this is why you came.*

Thank you, Jesus, for being willing to come.

Independence Day | **July 4**

Bird brains
Jason Nelson

I can tell the bright red cardinal coming to my bird feeder is irritated with me. Apparently, I didn't get the seed placement to his liking. I neglected to shake the bag to mix the seed. I just poured it into the feeder. So the sunflower seeds that were at the bottom of the bag are at the top of the feeder. And cardinals really like those. I watch him sift through and spit out all the little round seeds only the sparrows will eat. *Pthewy. Pthewy, Pthewy.* Then he glares at me through the window, raises a wing, and flips me the feather. Even birds are fussy eaters.

Abundance is a mixed blessing. If we were born in the U.S., we might take its bounty for granted. This land, your land, my land is a big, beautiful, generous place with a wide-open heartland. It is still a rising star in the constellation of human societies. Because I live here, **"I will sing the Lord's praise, for he has been good to me"** (Psalm 13:6).

O beautiful for spacious skies, for amber waves of grain,
For purple mountain majesties above the fruited plain!
America! America!
God shed His grace on thee,
And crown thy good with brotherhood
From sea to shining sea! (Katharine Lee Bates)

That showy cardinal could take a lesson from the humble sparrows. They take the tiny seeds, line up shoulder to shoulder on my railing, and sing.

July 5

Your job description
Linda Buxa

My son's head football coach held an online meeting for parents. While he was introducing himself and the other members of the coaching staff, he said something that caught my attention. He told us he had found people with "low ego, high output—who the real ones are."

I immediately realized that God wants the same kind of people on his team.

A church leader named Paul wrote a letter to believers who lived in a city called Philippi. He shared how to have low ego and high output: **"Make my joy complete by being like-minded, having the same love, being one in spirit and of one mind. Do nothing out of selfish ambition or vain conceit. Rather, in humility value others above yourselves, not looking to your own interests but each of you to the interests of the others"** (Philippians 2:2-4).

Right before he died, Jesus shared another part of the job description: **"As I have loved you, so you must love one another. By this everyone will know that you are my disciples, if you love one another"** (John 13:34,35).

People who follow Jesus are on Team Jesus, and God—our head coach—wants us to work together, serve others, love God, love people, be humble, be self-sacrificing, follow Jesus' example.

P.S. This isn't something we do to earn God's approval. We already have his approval because God has given us new hearts and transformed our minds. This is what makes it possible for "real" Christians to have low ego and high output.

July 6

Let God's strong people serve you
Matt Trotter

Second Corinthians 11 has a wild ending, a strong apostle boasting in his weakness: **"If I must boast, I will boast of the things that show my weakness. The God and Father of the Lord Jesus, who is to be praised forever, knows that I am not lying. In Damascus the governor under King Aretas had the city of the Damascenes guarded in order to arrest me. But I was lowered in a basket from a window in the wall and slipped through his hands"** (verses 30-33).

Paul, recounting for the congregation at Corinth, shares his escape from arrest. He tells them how he had to crawl out of a window and be let down in a basket!

I do think it proves a point though. Paul had taken beatings and imprisonment to share the gospel. He was a strong, able missionary. Yet for his escape, he had to be weak and sneak. Someone had to lower that basket. Probably two strong believers selected a strong basket, climbed on a roof, tied a rope, picked up an apostle, and became a human-powered elevator. They were strong; Paul was powerless.

As a believer in Jesus, be open to people helping you. Trust the small and daring things that can change the course of the world. When strong people want to help your weak self out of a tough situation, be willing to say, "Yes!" even when the basket is itchy, tight, or small. God's strength will be shown in your weakness.

July 7

Dice, Legos, and God's love of community
Mike Novotny

My family and I play a game where you have to (1) roll ten dice until they all match and then (2) stack those ten dice in a vertical tower. I am impressively fast at (1) and frustratingly bad at (2). My towers always lean, wobble, and topple over.

That's why I like Legos better. Give me ten Legos, ask me to stack them up, and I will lock one on top of the other into a straight and solid tower. You can knock the table and even huff and puff your strongest breath, but that Lego tower will stay standing.

Why am I telling you this? Because too many churches are too much like the dice and too little like the Legos. Christians are close to each other, but they are not truly connected to each other. We sit close at our church services and fellowship events, but we don't get connected to each other as God intends.

How do we become more like Legos? One of my favorite passages says, **"Therefore confess your sins to each other and pray for each other so that you may be healed"** (James 5:16). I have seen near strangers get deeply connected through this kind of confession. In fact, it happens in my living room when our small group gathers together. We push ourselves to honesty, even when it's momentarily embarrassing, and God responds with the blessing of true Christian fellowship and spiritual healing.

Please don't spend the next year of your life just close to other Christians. It's time to get truly connected!

July 8

Best day ever
Liz Schroeder

I decided to make today the best day ever, and I've found confirmation everywhere I look. I've never seen the mountains look this way with the cloud formations just so—the best day ever! A friend shared the good news that she has been drug free for one year—thank you, Lord! I was privileged to hold, feed, and burp a friend's newborn baby—best day ever! I met up with another friend to hike a trail that was new to me. It was more challenging than either of us expected. A fall could be deadly, in which case, "Hello, heaven!"—best day ever.

This is far from toxic positivity, which involves disconnecting from true feelings and forcing a good mood. This is simply what happens when we open our eyes to the ways God blesses us every day. Psalm 9:1,2 says, **"I will give thanks to you, Lord, with all my heart; I will tell of all your wonderful deeds. I will be glad and rejoice in you; I will sing praises of your name, O Most High."**

The God who formed the mountains and paints the skies is the same God who formed you. He feeds you and holds you and keeps your foot from slipping.

"Let the peace of Christ rule in your hearts, since as members of one body you were called to peace. And be thankful" (Colossians 3:15).

With a heart full of gratitude and the peace of Christ, today is truly the best day ever. And so is tomorrow.

July 9

Rid your heart of jealousy
Mike Novotny

If Jesus put slander on the same list as murder, adultery, and theft (Matthew 15:19), why are hurtful, untrue words so tempting for us?

Here's one reason—jealousy. I remember being jealous of a fellow pastor whose church seemed to be doing better than mine. One day I heard that this pastor put in long hours at church. My sinful heart took that fact and jumped to the slanderous conclusion: "He's *probably* a bad husband and not there for his kids." Did I have evidence of that? No. But that assumption helped me feel better about me, which was really about my jealousy and insecurity.

Jealousy will tempt you too. Why did he make the team and you didn't? The coach *probably* played favorites. Why does she get the guys' attention? She *probably* spends a lot on her looks. Why did he get the job? *Probably* because . . . (fill in unsubstantiated reason to deal with your insecurity). When someone gets something you want, beware that jealousy doesn't lead you into slander.

"Anger is cruel and fury overwhelming, but who can stand before jealousy?" (Proverbs 27:4). If jealousy is hijacking your heart and overflowing your lips, run to Jesus. In his grace, he will forgive your verbal sins and insecure assumptions and offer you the antidote—himself. If God is for you, beside you, within you, you don't need the starting spot, the boss' praise, or any other blessing.

I pray that Jesus can rid your heart of jealousy so your words are full of grace and truth.

July 10

But then
C.L. Whiteside

People love the biblical accounts of Ruth, Joseph, and Job. Their stories resonate because each of them endured serious hardship but ultimately experienced a happy ending. Ruth lost her husband, remained faithful to her mother-in-law, but then found her Prince Charming in Boaz. Joseph was sold into slavery, falsely accused of rape, and thrown into prison, yet he eventually became second-in-command in the greatest nation of his time. Job lost almost everything, but then God blessed him with twice as many possessions as he had before.

But what if there was no "but then" in these stories? Would being a child of God still be worth it? The answer is an overwhelming yes! You are showered in God's grace through faith in Jesus Christ, and if you believe, it wouldn't matter if another good thing or earthly blessing ever came your way because salvation is so much greater.

Mark 8:36 reminds us, **"What good is it for someone to gain the whole world, yet forfeit their soul?"** Most of us aren't trying to gain the whole world—we just want to be comfortable and live decent lives, right? But no earthly treasure or pleasure is worth your salvation. And no hardship or obstacle in this life compares to the horror of hell and eternal separation from God.

There is always a "but then" for a believer. It may look different from what you imagine and not be a big earthly pleasure, but remember that spending eternity with your heavenly Father is worth it—oh, so worth it!

July 11

Determination
Matt Ewart

Nehemiah had every reason to stay where he was. But a strong conviction created an unstoppable determination. It was the fifth century B.C. He was a Jewish exile who served in the Persian king's palace far from his homeland of Jerusalem, which lay in ruins. He had a stable position as the king's cupbearer, but an inner conviction grew so strong that it compelled him to take on an incredible challenge.

Burdened for his people, Nehemiah boldly asked the king for permission to return to Jerusalem and rebuild it. He rallied workers, led through opposition, and persevered against threats. Despite the challenges, he never wavered. Nehemiah rebuilt the walls of Jerusalem, not because the task was easy but because a strong conviction created unstoppable determination.

Where did his conviction come from? It was anchored in a promise from God: **"If you return to me and obey my commands, then . . . I will gather them from there and bring them to the place I have chosen as a dwelling for my Name"** (Nehemiah 1:9).

You have promises from God too. His conviction was to love you, and it led to an unstoppable determination to save you. Jesus faced opposition, endured a cross, and overcame sin and death for you. Now you are part of his kingdom—a **"living stone"** in his **"spiritual house"** (1 Peter 2:5).

When challenges arise or when God's way isn't the easy way, remember the promises that accompany you. A strong conviction in God's promises will create an unstoppable determination to follow him.

July 12

The gift of a *kenzoku*
Jan Gompper

According to my Facebook statistics, I have 1,400 friends. You may have far more. I couldn't name them all, and some I've had very little (if any) communication with—ever! Today's world puts a lot of emphasis on social media connections, termed "friends." Having lots of followers or friends is supposed to validate us somehow. But do they really?

The Japanese have a term for friend—*kenzoku*. Literally translated it means "family." This implies a bond of deep connection—a comradeship.

I remember having a few such *kenzokus* in college. We would stay up until the wee hours of the morning discussing careers, love, dreams, politics, faith. I miss those days. This kind of friendship requires an investment of time and vulnerability—a willingness to share and listen without judgment—a willingness to debate, disagree, and still love.

David and Saul's son Jonathan had such a friendship. Although Saul was jealous and fearful of David, **"Jonathan made a covenant with David because he loved him as himself"** (1 Samuel 18:3). When Jonathan was killed in battle, David lamented: **"I grieve for you, Jonathan my brother; you were very dear to me. Your love for me was wonderful, more wonderful than that of women"** (2 Samuel 1:26). Their friendship was deep and selfless, having greater intimacy than even a sexual relationship.

One of my favorite passages about friendship comes from Proverbs 27:9—A sweet friendship refreshes the soul.

Having 1,400+ friends on Facebook may feed our egos, but having a *kenzoku* feeds our souls.

July 13

God goes before you
Nathan Nass

God goes before you. I know it doesn't always feel that way, but God always goes before you.

He showed his people that in a powerful way in the Old Testament. As God led the Israelites from Egypt to the Promised Land, **"the Lord went ahead of them in a pillar of cloud to guide them on their way and by night in a pillar of fire to give them light, so that they could travel by day or night. Neither the pillar of cloud by day nor the pillar of fire by night left its place in front of the people"** (Exodus 13:21,22).

That must have been so comforting, don't you think? Day or night, they could see that God went before them. Through the desert. Through the mountains. Through the sea. All the way to the Promised Land.

God goes before you too. I know you can't see his presence in a pillar of fire or in a cloud, but God goes before you too. That's his promise! Jesus is with you always. God is aware of all that is happening in your life. There is meaning and purpose in everything that happens.

God goes before you. Through the dry, desert times. Through the mountaintop moments. Through the highs and lows. Through the pains and joys. He's there. Beside you. All the time. All the way. He's leading you through this wilderness to the Promised Land of heaven by faith in Jesus. God goes before you!

July 14

You and two lions
Daron Lindemann

Are you ready to cross paths with a lion? Actually, two lions?

Each of us encounters a lion known as the devil. **"Your enemy the devil prowls around like a roaring lion looking for someone to devour. Resist him, standing firm in the faith"** (1 Peter 5:8,9).

The devil uses his lies to scare you away from Jesus, and if you believe him—if you let him stalk between you and Jesus—you'll be his lunch.

But another lion crosses your path. Bigger than the first lion, this lion never lies and his Word is always true. This lion knows you better than the first lion. This lion has battle scars but has never lost a fight and never will.

"'Do not weep! See, the Lion of the tribe of Judah . . . has triumphed' . . . a Lamb, looking as if it had been slain, standing at the center of the throne" (Revelation 5:5,6).

Jesus is both Lion and Lamb, both King and Servant, both Warrior and Sacrifice. Like a sacrificial lamb, Jesus died for the sins of the world. Like a predator lion, Jesus rose from the dead with all authority over heaven and earth.

He is the real Lion King.

Dear Jesus, be my Lion. When the lies of the devil roar, when fears stalk me in the night, when I'm tempted, or when I'm surrounded by enemies, use your ferocious power. Deliver me from them and from my own weakness, sin, and small faith. Amen.

July 15

Outrage isn't our theology
Jason Nelson

Are you as exhausted with outrage as I am? It seems like people want to cook it up over just about anything. Politicians on both sides of the aisle take their turn revving up the outrage machine to fire up supporters. Some religious leaders preach on with self-righteous indignation. The poor cable guy gets an earful over bad reception. Celebrities get ripped on social media because someone is outraged over the garish things they wore. The outrage of Pharisees got Jesus killed. Outrage can ignite full-blown rage.

Friends of Jesus, let us express ourselves without outrage, because outrage is not our theology. We can say the tough things in God's Holy Word without hatred. Our sincere hearts should be evident to all. We can have a quieting influence in a boisterous world if we emphasize the same things that Jesus did.

Jesus confronted evil with righteous wrath but not by ranting in rage. And when he taught as one having God's authority, he delivered good news. Actually, he delivered perfect news of peace, mercy, forgiveness, comfort, and righteousness. The talking points in his most famous sermon (Mathew 5-7) may sound surreal to us today, but he meant every word of it. He insisted that we live that way and that we show others how to live that way.

That kind of talk irked a lot of people, so they nailed him to a cross. From that cross he said without outrage, **"Father, forgive them, for they do not know what they are doing"** (Luke 23:34).

July 16

It's better than OK
Nate Wordell

What's the difference between saying, "I forgive you" and saying, "It's okay"?

If your friend's elbow touches yours, she might apologize. But it would be weird if you pulled in close, lowered your voice, and said, "From the bottom of my heart, I forgive you." That's an "it's OK" moment because "it's OK" means "no harm done."

But sometimes harm *is* done between friends. She trashed your reputation. He took credit for your work. They excluded you. It would be weird to pretend that things are OK. So God invented the other phrase. "I forgive you" is like saying, "Your action cost me something, and I could get it back if I choose revenge—but I won't. You don't owe me."

When Jesus taught us how to pray, he gave us these words: **"Forgive us our debts, as we also have forgiven our debtors"** (Matthew 6:12).

When we cross one of God's lines, he doesn't say, "It's OK." He says: "Harm done. I wanted to be united with you—one mind and heart—but you broke that. You cost us our beautiful relationship." Then he says: "I forgive you. I will cover the cost to repair our relationship. You don't owe me anything." Jesus didn't teach it only; he accomplished it when he paid for all our sins with his death and resurrection.

And as soon as he was back from the grave, he gave you his power. **"If you forgive anyone's sins, their sins are forgiven"** (John 20:23).

It's not just OK; it's forgiven.

Best for the best
Matt Ewart

It can be easy to be kind to people you only see occasionally. A smile, a compliment, or a polite gesture can come naturally when you're around casual acquaintances or total strangers.

But when you're with the people who know you best, the unpolished version of you comes out. Patience wears thin. Harshness becomes the default. A "me first" mindset takes over. Kindness is a struggle.

Why do the people we know least often get our best? And why do the people we know best often get our worst? While I can't explain the psychology behind it, I can point to the solution for it: **"Let us not become weary in doing good, for at the proper time we will reap a harvest if we do not give up. Therefore, as we have opportunity, let us do good to all people, especially to those who belong to the family of believers"** (Galatians 6:9,10).

God knows us completely. He knows the unpolished version of who we really are—weaknesses, failures, and all. Yet despite what he knows, he still loves us with his very best. He gave his one and only Son.

Today, make an intentional effort to give your best to those who know you best. The kind word, "you first" gesture, or gentle smile that you're so willing to give to a stranger—give that to someone at home too. They might not always see the polished version of you, but today let them see the forgiven version of you.

July 18

Money is powerful
Mike Novotny

My wife and I bought our youngest daughter her first smartphone for her 15th birthday. She might have been the last kid in her class to get one, not because Kim and I believe that phones are bad but because we have experienced that phones are powerful. Your attention span, friendships, mental health, faith life, and so much more are radically affected by those ever-present devices.

That's why before we handed over that powerful digital rectangle, we talked to our daughter. A lot.

Money is like that. Money isn't inherently good or bad, but it is extraordinarily powerful. Money can increase your worry or feed the poor, pull you away from church or get the gospel to new people and places, bless families with memorable road trips or tear them apart in bitter inheritance squabbles. That's why our Father wants to talk to you about money. A lot.

I recently learned that the words *offering, gold, silver, money, greed/greedy,* and *generous/generosity* show up in the Bible more times than the name of Jesus! Given that frequency and the power of money, I hope you are open to conversations, sermons, and devotions that connect faith and finances. Yes, we should be very wary of money-loving clergy, but let's not swing to the opposite extreme and stay silent about something as powerful as finances.

Pray that the Spirit would give you ears to hear the next time your Father wants to talk about the powerful gift of money. May your heart reply, **"I rejoice in following your statutes as one rejoices in great riches"** (Psalm 119:14).

July 19

On recognition
Liz Schroeder

It's annoying to be locked out of an account you need to access. You have to get a new password. First, enter the login code sent to your email and the verification code sent via text. Then, create a strong password and reenter it. Finally, pray that it works.

It's not only annoying not to be recognized; it can be downright hurtful. Have you experienced the pain of a classmate walking past you without acknowledging your existence? Or when a kid in your church who used to run up and give you a hug is now a teenager who won't look you in the eye?

What I am learning is that every twinge of pain gives me a window into the suffering that Jesus endured on this earth. Jesus' closest friends, and even his cousin John the Baptist, didn't recognize him for who he was. Surely the Savior of the world would be more impressive and wouldn't hang out with tax collectors and prostitutes. Certainly the Messiah would act more militant and make the Roman army shake in their sandals.

When John sent his disciples to Jesus to find out if he was the Messiah, **"Jesus replied, 'Go back and report to John what you hear and see: The blind receive sight . . . the dead are raised, and the good news is proclaimed to the poor. Blessed is anyone who does not stumble on account of me'"** (Matthew 11:4-6).

What's it going to take for you to recognize Jesus Christ's lordship in your life?

July 20

The key to growing in love
Dave Scharf

As Christians, we want to be more loving to others. No one would say that we can't grow in putting others before ourselves. Knowledge is the key. The apostle Paul says, **"This is my prayer: that your love may abound more and more in knowledge and depth of insight"** (Philippians 1:9). Of course, the key is not just knowing *things* better but rather knowing *Jesus* better.

Paul says later in this letter, **"I want to know Christ"** (3:10). Jesus knows you. He knows you better than you know yourself. He knows everything, even those things you've never told anyone that would make you unlovable to everyone who knew. And Jesus loves you anyway. I want to *know* that love. I want to spend the rest of my life digging down to the depths of what would drive Jesus to leave heaven for earth, glory for filth, eternal happiness for eternal hell on a cross. Do you want to know what drove him? It's you. *"I want to know Christ."*

Knowing Christ is more than just knowing the facts. It's experiencing them. It's a relationship with Jesus. How good of a relationship would you have if you only spoke to your significant other once a month? That wouldn't be a strong relationship! There's no way you could really *know* each other! The same is true with knowing Jesus. Spend time getting to know Jesus' love in his Word every day. That's the key to growing in love.

July 21

You need only to be still
Nathan Nass

God's Old Testament people panicked. Have you ever had panicky moments? Your heart races. You feel helpless.

For the Israelites, the problem was that they were trapped. They had just escaped slavery in Egypt by God's grace and the power of the ten plagues, but soon they found themselves trapped between the Red Sea on one side and charging Egyptian chariots on the other.

The Israelites panicked. Terrified, they cried out to the Lord and to Moses: **"What have you done to us by bringing us out of Egypt?"** (Exodus 14:11).

Moses replied with these amazing, calming words: **"The Lord will fight for you; you need only to be still"** (Exodus 14:14). What did the Israelites need to do to rescue themselves from their predicament? Nothing. Just be still. They weren't the ones who would fight. The Lord was. The Lord would fight for them. And he did. God parted the waters of the Red Sea, let the Israelites cross on dry ground, and then drowned the Egyptians under the waves.

"The Lord will fight for you; you need only to be still." That's true for you too! The biggest battles in life aren't fought by you. The Lord fights for you. We're all helpless against sin, death, hell, and guilt. But Jesus fought for us and won for us and saved us.

When panic starts to set in, tell yourself these amazing, calming words: "The Lord will fight for you; you need only to be still."

July 22

What a miracle!
Jon Enter

Do you know the story of James Bartley? In 1891 he was harpooning a whale, fell overboard, and was swallowed alive by it. His fellow fishermen caught the whale. When they cut open its belly, James was alive! He had spent 36 hours in that near-death tomb.

Some doubt this actually happened. But the prophet Jonah knew how it felt. He spent three days and nights in the belly of a great fish after he defied God and tried sailing away from Nineveh, where God had commanded him to preach. But God's will is always done, and the Lord sent a nautical Uber to redirect Jonah to his heavenly mission.

Jonah didn't want to go because he didn't think the Ninevites deserved God's grace. **"I tried to forestall by fleeing to Tarshish. I knew that you are a gracious and compassionate God . . . a God who relents from sending calamity"** (Jonah 4:2). Isn't it surprising that God's prophet didn't want the God of grace to show grace?

Whom do you know who doesn't deserve grace? Who needs to "get theirs"? Who makes you feel awful about yourself or callously crushed you?

It's hard to show mercy to the merciless, but that's what God does for you. Your God is "gracious and compassionate." That's how God treats you. That's how God calls you to treat others. Maybe when you treat others with grace as God treats you, their hearts might be changed to know Jesus' mercy and to treat you differently.

July 23

America's #1 belief
Mike Novotny

America's #1 belief is "basically me spirituality." Picture it like a big buffet of all kinds of beliefs. You like Jesus' forgiveness? Then take a big serving. Don't like Jesus' fire and brimstone? You can skip to the next dish. You're into "there's a reason for everything"? Let's take two scoops of that. Not so into "confess your sins to one another"? No worries. Mix and match the messages that you like most. That's "basically me spirituality."

I can see why some would want to believe that. It feels freeing. Empowering. It avoids some of the corruption of a religious institution and the hypocrisy of man-made rules. But if I could ask you to reconsider, today I'd like to invite you to a better kind of belief that I call better-than-me Christianity.

King David proclaimed this faith when he wrote: **"Keep me safe, my God, for in you I take refuge. I say to the Lord, 'You are my Lord; apart from you I have no good thing'"** (Psalm 16:1,2). David's ultimate authority was clearly not David but instead the one he labeled "God," "Lord," and "Lord." But David wasn't pouty about living under God's authority, because this God kept him safe. This Lord blessed him with every good thing.

Jesus is offering you something better than a DIY faith or an "empowering" buffet of beliefs. He is offering you God! That God insists on keeping his authority, but he will bless you with eternal safety.

Nothing matters more than that.

July 24

Holding up the prophet's hands
Nathan Nass

You can't do it all yourself. Do you need that reminder today? We get bombarded with messages about how "independent" and "strong" we are. We get it in our heads that we don't need anybody for anything.

That's not true. You can't do it all yourself. Even Moses couldn't. As Moses led God's people to the Promised Land, the Israelites were attacked by the Amalekites. As Joshua led the army into battle, Moses stood on a mountain with his arms raised. As long as Moses' arms were raised, their army won.

But Moses couldn't do it all himself. Of course, the power for the victory came from the Lord. But Moses couldn't even hold his arms up by himself. **"When Moses' hands grew tired, they took a stone and put it under him and he sat on it. Aaron and Hur held his hands up—one on one side, one on the other—so that his hands remained steady till sunset"** (Exodus 17:12). Moses needed someone to hold up his hands.

You do too. You can't do it all yourself. First and foremost, you need Jesus, your Savior, to give you forgiveness and grace and strength each day. Every victory comes from Jesus! But like Moses, you also need other Christians to hold you up, just like other Christians need you to support and encourage them.

You can't do it all yourself, and you don't have to! Jesus teaches his people to hold up each others' hands.

July 25

Take comfort in Baptism
Jan Gompper

When the first automobiles were manufactured, only the very wealthy could afford one. Now pretty much every family has one in the U.S. The same is true of televisions, computers, cell phones.

Do you know what else almost every family has today? Someone who is suffering from some form of mental illness or addiction or both. You can see it in the weary countenances of grandparents raising their grandchildren or in the teary eyes of parents who have a child they no longer know how to help.

The most grievous thing for Christian parents of a mentally ill or addiction-riddled child is wondering whether their son or daughter will be in heaven. To those burdened by this worry, take heart by remembering: **"When God our Savior revealed his kindness and love, he saved us, not because of the righteous things we had done, but because of his mercy. He washed away our sins, giving us a new birth and new life through the Holy Spirit. He generously poured out the Spirit upon us through Jesus Christ our Savior. Because of his grace he made us right in his sight and gave us confidence that we will inherit eternal life"** (Titus 3:4-7 NLT).

Mental illness or addiction does not negate what God did for them at their baptism—he made them his children. The Holy Spirit has brought them to saving faith, and he can keep them in that faith. As God's precious children, nothing can snatch them out of his hand.

July 26

Do dogs go to heaven?
Matt Ewart

One of the most common questions I get from my middle school students is, "Will my dog be in heaven?"

The question was so common one year that I decided to spend an entire lesson on the topic. We started the lesson by talking about how awesome dogs are. (Sorry, cat people.) Students shared stories of their beloved pets, and the room was filled with warm fuzzies—until I dropped this truth: *Not everyone likes dogs.* (You're welcome, cat people.) Some people are afraid of them, and others have a greater love for different animals. Some people have pet tarantulas. Others have pet snakes. Guess what *they* hope makes it to heaven?

I get it. Pets are wonderful blessings from God, offering us love and companionship. It's natural to want what we love most to be with us in heaven. But if everyone wanted heaven to include everything they love on earth, it would not be a very good heaven for any of us.

Maybe God's **"new heaven and new earth"** (Revelation 21:1) will have pets. The Bible doesn't say specifically. But I do know this: Once we're in heaven, God's presence will be so overwhelming that we won't even think about looking for the pets we had here on earth.

Heaven will have what God loves the most: you and me.

"Therefore, 'they are before the throne of God and serve him day and night in his temple; and he who sits on the throne will shelter them with his presence'" (Revelation 7:15).

July 27

Why did God make science?
Nate Wordell

It's pretty obvious why God made the stars in the night sky. **"The heavens declare the glory of God; the skies proclaim the work of his hands"** (Psalm 19:1). It's clear why God made so many tasty plants. **"God said, 'I give you every seed-bearing plant on the face of the whole earth and every tree that has fruit with seed in it. They will be yours for food'"** (Genesis 1:29). Animals too. **"Everything that lives and moves about will be food for you. Just as I gave you the green plants, I now give you everything"** (Genesis 9:3).

But why did God make our natural world observable, measurable, predictable, studyable, and manipulatable? He could care for our universe with miracles all the time and no explanation. Instead, God made science. Why?

Because just like the sky and plants and animals are gifts for you, science is too. Science is one of the greatest ways for God to love you and for you to love your neighbor.

Jesus' classic lesson in how to love is the story of the good Samaritan. It's all recorded in Luke 10. The good man used science to analyze a man's injuries, medicine to provide first-century first aid, and even math to calculate the cost of the man's care.

God is still sending good Samaritans to research, engineer, nurse, and care for the people he loves. It's yet another way the love of God makes it through human hands right to you.

July 28

God listens to hesitant believers
Linda Buxa

There's a story in the Bible about a man named Lot who lived in Sodom and Gomorrah, a place where the people's sins were so offensive that God was planning to incinerate the area. Angels told Lot to run, but **"when he hesitated, the men grasped his hand and the hands of his wife and of his two daughters and led them safely out of the city, for the Lord was merciful to them"** (Genesis 19:16).

The angels told them to escape to the mountains, but Lot replied, **"I can't flee to the mountains; this disaster will overtake me, and I'll die"** (verse 19). He asked to run to a nearby town instead. Astonishingly, the angels agreed. Wait a minute! The guy who needed angels to grab his hands to save his life had the courage to ask to escape to a different place than he had been told—and they said yes?!

Astonishingly, I'm actually comforted by this. See, there have been times when I've had a fearful faith and have hesitated when I know what God says to do. It might be tempting to think I've lost the right to pray boldly to the King of the universe, but I haven't, and neither have you. That's because our right to approach our God is not about our hesitant hearts but about the faithfulness of a God who calls us his children and tells us to **"approach God's throne of grace with confidence, so that we may receive mercy and find grace to help us in our time of need"** (Hebrews 4:16).

July 29

Let God be God
C.L. Whiteside

Trusting God can be extremely difficult when we don't understand the why. Why did God let this person die? Why am I suffering in this way? These are the kinds of why questions we all wrestle with at times.

Sometimes God chooses to reveal things to us. Other times he makes us wait, and we don't know why. In those moments, we must remember he is perfect, just, loving, compassionate, all-knowing, and merciful. We can lean on passages like John 13:7, where Jesus told his disciples, **"You do not realize now what I am doing, but later you will understand."**

We can also look to examples like Jonah, who didn't understand God's plan. Jonah was angry that God spared a city Jonah believed was too evil to be saved.

The account of Job is another example people turn to when struggling. Job lost all his wealth and children, and his health was cursed terribly due to him being tested. Many love this story because God ultimately blessed the latter part of Job's life more than the first. However, most forget that when Job asked God why, God responded by essentially saying in Job 40-42: "Job, do you know who I am? Do you know what I've done? I am God—now I'll ask you the questions!" Job's transformation is one we can seek to emulate. He went from challenging God's fairness to repenting and standing in awe of God's patience and power.

God's integrity is perfect. There will be times when we simply need to let God be God.

July 30

Why me, Lord?
Ann Jahns

I'm a pretty disciplined person. In fact, when I take strengths assessments, "discipline" ranks in my top five. Except when it comes to writing these devotions. I can procrastinate like a pro. Suddenly there are things I have to do—like reorganize my desk drawers or sharpen all the pencils in the house.

Why the procrastination? Maybe because writing is hard. Or—more likely—because I don't feel qualified. Who am I, a sinner, to encourage or challenge anyone else in their spiritual life?

The Bible is filled with people who asked, "Why me, Lord?" When God tasked Moses with persuading Pharaoh to let the Israelites leave Egypt, we can almost picture Moses wringing his hands as he offered excuses: **"Pardon your servant, Lord. I have never been eloquent. . . . I am slow of speech and tongue"** (Exodus 4:10). But look how God responded: **"Who gave human beings their mouths? . . . Is it not I, the Lord? Now go; I will help you speak and will teach you what to say"** (verses 11,12).

Have you ever felt like Moses? Unqualified or ill-equipped or uncomfortable in sharing your faith? You're not alone. If God chose only the perfectly qualified for his outreach team, there would be no team. Are you a perfect Christian? No. Will you say the perfect words in every situation? Unlikely. But take courage! God's Holy Spirit lives in you and will equip you.

Remember, God will help you speak and teach you what to say. He has promised it!

July 31

Our version of Greek gods
Mike Novotny

Do you ever wonder where the ancient gods came from? Here's my theory: People simply personalized the deepest longings of their hearts. For example, people wanted power and control over the chaos of the world, so they named him Zeus and prayed for his blessing. Others wanted beauty, romance, and the feeling of falling in love, so they called her Aphrodite and sacrificed to appease her. Others ached for the way art could touch the soul, so they dubbed him Apollo and hoped he would smile upon them. In our day, we don't use the same names, but we still long for the same things—control, beauty, emotion, family, safety, money, escape.

But these cravings can be spiritually dangerous. Not only are they not true gods, but they demand costly sacrifices. If your ultimate passion is family or work or being right or looking good or being praised, what good things will end up on the altar? What sacrifices will you have to make? How will it affect your relationship with God and his Word?

Our Lord once lamented, **"These men have set up idols in their hearts"** (Ezekiel 14:3). Knowing how much these gods will cost you (and how they don't even exist!), the true God calls us to repent and turn back to him. Let good things be good things and never godlike things that we need to be content.

Only Yahweh is worthy of such praise because he is the only God who exists, the only God who loves, the only God who saves.

AUGUST

Children's children are a crown to the aged,
and parents are the pride of their children.

PROVERBS 17:6

August 1

The #1 reason you need other Christians
Mike Novotny

I walked wearily into my home, dragging after a marathon day of work. Before I tucked my daughters into bed, I made the mistake of looking at my email, which contained a loooong critique of my ministry. It was written in love, I will admit, but it was also hard to take, especially when my energy level was low.

My daughter asked me what had happened. After I explained the situation, she responded, "Dad, you shouldn't be proud, but you should remember that not everyone feels that way about you. And don't forget that Jesus loves you!" (Man, I love that kid!)

Curious, I asked, "Thank you, sweetie. Is that what you tell yourself when someone criticizes you?"

Immediately her chin dropped, and she avoided my eyes. She shook her head sheepishly, her admission that it's much easier to tell the truth to others than to yourself.

There are many reasons our Father wants you to live in Christian community, but perhaps near the top of his list is our universal need to have others preach the gospel to us. When you sin, it can be so hard to tell yourself that Jesus forgives you, that you don't need to drag around your shame. But your fellow Christians will give you the gospel: "[Jesus] **is the atoning sacrifice for our sins, and not only for ours but also for the sins of the whole world**" (1 John 2:2).

If someone confesses a sin to you, give them the basics that might suddenly seem hard to believe. I pray they can do the same for you.

August 2

Changing your morning mood
Liz Schroeder

Feeling tense today? We're going to listen to some music together, but first take a look at these verb tenses: **"I am certain that God, who began the good work within you, will continue his work until it is finished on the day when Christ Jesus returns"** (Philippians 1:6 NLT).

"I am" = present, "began" = past, "will continue" = future. You can be certain of heaven now because of the good work God has done in you in the past and will continue until Jesus returns. God's got your past, present, and future. His work within you is ongoing, sustaining. In musical terms, it's *legato*, not *staccato*.

Think of the quintessential staccato song "Chopsticks." It's disjointed, detached. And then there's "Morning Mood" by Edvard Grieg. (Go ahead and pull up the song.) The notes are legato, tied together with no silence between them. Do you hear how the flute and oboe trade phrases seamlessly? The rest of the orchestra swells as the violins take the melody until the brass players can barely restrain themselves. As the final chord resolves, can you imagine all of creation applauding the sunrise?

God's work in your life is "Morning Mood," not "Chopsticks." Even when it feels like he is silent or events seem disjointed and purposeless, your Father is conducting a symphony, tying all things together for your good (Romans 8:28). When you're feeling tense, remember who is orchestrating all things from your past and present into a glorious resolution at Christ's return.

August 3

Jesus & money
Mike Novotny

If you get nervous when your pastor brings up money, consider how frequently Jesus did it. In more than half of his parables, Jesus used explicitly financial language.

For example, to teach us to love our neighbor, Jesus told the parable of the good Samaritan, a kind stranger who gave *money* to cover the medical bills of a man he found on the side of a road. To save us from materialism, Jesus told the parable of a *rich* fool, a shortsighted man who thought more about storage for his stuff than his salvation or soul. To inspire us with God's passion to save us, Jesus told the parable of the lost *coin*, how God incessantly searches to find you when you are far from him. To remind us of how glorious God is, Jesus told the parable of the hidden *treasure*, which teaches that God is the greatest treasure of all. And for those of us who lament the ways we have sinned financially, Jesus told the parable of the Pharisee and the *tax* collector, the latter who cried for mercy and received it from a merciful God.

It is good to talk about money because that's what Jesus did many times. **"Therefore go and make disciples of all nations, baptizing them in the name of the Father and of the Son and of the Holy Spirit, and teaching them to obey everything I have commanded you"** (Matthew 28:19,20). May our hearts be open as Jesus teaches us how to handle the precious gift of money.

August 4

Even now
Matt Ewart

Life is a book, and each chapter has its highs and lows. Some chapters bring exciting new opportunities, such as graduating, landing your dream job, or welcoming a grandchild. These moments feel like the beginning of something great.

But sometimes the chapter ends before you'd like it to. Sometimes the life you're planning for ends abruptly, leaving you to grieve the harsh reality of something lost. Life is a book of highs and lows, filled with unexpected twists.

Martha experienced one of those difficult chapters in John 11:22 when she spoke to Jesus: **"I know that *even now* God will give you whatever you ask."** She was in the middle of a deep sorrow, grieving the loss of her brother, Lazarus. Yet in that moment of mourning, she expressed faith in God's power and presence. Her "even now" was bad, but she knew Jesus would get her through it.

You will have those "even now" moments too. Unexpected loss can open up so much uncertainty and pain. When those times come, *even now* in the midst of your grief or fear, God is at work. He can bring hope into your despair and make a way where there seems to be no way.

Every chapter of life, whether joyous or sorrowful, is a part of God's bigger story. He lovingly and faithfully walks with you through each chapter. Even now, he is present, working in ways you may not always understand. Trust that his plan is good, even now.

August 5

Power tools
Daron Lindemann

I rented a hydraulic log splitter. It was straining hard to split bigger logs, so I pulled hard on the lever for more power. It split—not the log, but the log splitter. The metal cracked.

I also drove my riding lawnmower off a curb. Instead of driving 30 feet on the street to use the driveway to get back on my lawn, I tried to lift the lawnmower over the curb. My thigh pushed up against the hot carburetor. The smell of burning skin and the sting of pain made me scream, and now I have a scar about the size of a credit card.

Power tools are dangerous, but not by themselves. It's often operator error: usually carelessness of some kind and a combination of foolishness and pride.

We love power. Together with pride, we hurt ourselves, others, and God by using power words to hurt, making powerful decisions that benefit only us, and power shopping with credit we can't afford.

But there is a greater power—the power of Jesus Christ. **"To this end I strenuously contend with all the energy Christ so powerfully works in me"** (Colossians 1:29).

How are you using power in your life? What work is Jesus Christ doing with his power tools?

Dear Jesus, your power is greater than my pride and sin. I repent and come to you for the grace to use your power in my life instead of my own. Amen.

August 6

God did this
Nathan Nass

Whatever you're facing today, here's a comforting truth: God did this.

Even when life seems impossibly cruel. Have you heard the story of Joseph in the Bible? Joseph's ten older brothers were jealous of him, so they threw him into a pit. Then they sold him into slavery in Egypt. Sound good? It was awful! Joseph was rejected by his family and a slave in a foreign country.

It got worse. Joseph served his master faithfully, but he was accused falsely of attempted rape by his master's wife and thrown in prison. Joseph tried to help his fellow prisoners, but one of them forgot about him as soon as he got his freedom. Joseph's life seemed like a cursed failure.

Do you know who was behind all that? God. God did this! After years in prison, Joseph was released, saved the country from famine, and was promoted to second-in-command of all Egypt. Looking back over his life, Joseph told his brothers, **"It was not you who sent me here, but God"** (Genesis 45:8).

God did this. That's true for you too. Maybe today you're in a pit or have been unjustly accused. What you can't see is how God is working behind the scenes for your good. Maybe today you're in charge and feel like you're saving the world. What you can't see is how God is working behind the scenes to open doors for you. Like Joseph, learn to say, "God did this." You can trust in his plan!

August 7

A new identity
Dave Scharf

If you met God today, what would he say to you? If you are like me, you are painfully aware of the sins in your life. How could he not address you as sinner? But that's *not* how he would address you! When your parents told you growing up: "Remember who you are," they were reminding you of the responsibility and privilege of being part of a family. As a Christian, you have a new identity . . . a new family. The Bible says, **"You are all children of God . . . for all of you who were baptized into Christ have clothed yourselves with Christ"** (Galatians 3:26,27). When the Father looks at you, he sees one draped in the perfection of Jesus.

Your baptism is God's promise: "I will love you forever, no matter what." As Christians, I think it would be helpful to remember our baptisms at least twice a day, when we wake up and when we go to sleep, but for different reasons. When we wake up, we need to remember that God has given us a new identity in our baptisms, which affects how we act today. But then, before bed, we need to reflect on the day, admitting all the times we acted as though that name was not on us. We need to remember God's promise in our baptisms: "I washed it all away. I will love you forever, no matter what. You are my child, whom I love; with you, I am well pleased."

August 8

Justice for all
Nathan Nass

We like the idea of justice. We love it when people get punished as they deserve. We cheer when the bad guys get caught. As long as we're not the ones getting caught or punished.

We secretly hope justice never comes around to us. We proudly think that we are above the law. When the flashing lights pull over someone else, we think, "Finally. They deserved it!" When the flashing lights pull over you or me, we think, "No way! This isn't fair!"

The Bible has a wake-up call for us. God's justice is for all, because all have sinned: **"It will be the same for priest as for people, for the master as for his servant, for the mistress as for her servant, for seller as for buyer, for borrower as for lender, for debtor as for creditor"** (Isaiah 24:2). Don't ever think, "I'll get a pass. The rules are different for me." No! From the pastor to the people, God's justice is for all.

This is why we need Jesus! All of us need Jesus. Salvation doesn't come from our jobs or our money or our status. It comes through faith in Jesus. On the cross, Jesus bore the judgment we all deserve for our sins. Because of Jesus, here's God's promise: **"There is now no condemnation for those who are in Christ Jesus"** (Romans 8:1). God's justice is for all. So is Jesus' cross. We all need Jesus and his salvation!

August 9

Pride invites slander in
Mike Novotny

Slander is one of the many sins that ultimately stems from pride. Think how often pride takes a tough situation and blows it up with slanderous (a.k.a. untrue and/or unloving) words.

A frustrated wife yells, "You *never* think about what I want!" An angry husband snaps, "You *always* care more about the kids than me!" Never? Always? Neither of those statements is true, but the exaggeration makes the other person look like the problem and the only one who has changing to do.

That same pride twists memories and summaries of tense interactions. If you and I have a confrontational conversation, it will be tempting for me only to remember the worst thing you said (or how you said it). And you will be tempted to do the same when you tell your friend how the conversation went. When there's tension in a relationship, be very careful with your words, because pride wants to invite slander into the room.

Paul offers a better path: **"Do not let any unwholesome talk come out of your mouths, but only what is helpful for building others up according to their needs, that it may benefit those who listen"** (Ephesians 4:29).

This is how our Father speaks to us. His words, even when they cut deep and humble our hearts, are wholesome, helpful, and beneficial. They meet our deepest need of being saved and being right with God. Meditate on the way God has spoken to you, and then pray for his strength to speak the same way to those in your life.

August 10

Let's get our hands dirty
Ann Jahns

On December 29, 2025, former U.S. President Jimmy Carter died at the age of 100. Regardless of your opinion of his single term as president, no one can dispute the impact he made in his 50 years after leaving the Oval Office. Among his contributions was his hands-on, hammer-in-hand work for Habitat for Humanity, helping to renovate, restore, and build thousands of homes in more than a dozen countries for those needing help. Jimmy Carter got his hands dirty and put his love into action.

While on earth, Jesus displayed a level of hands-on love that was shocking to many. He wasn't afraid to get his hands dirty or sit with people in their pain or mess. Matthew says: **"Jesus went through all the towns and villages, teaching in their synagogues, proclaiming the good news of the kingdom and healing every disease and sickness. When he saw the crowds, he had compassion on them"** (9:35,36).

Jesus loved tax collectors, criminals, and prostitutes. His heart ached for the sick. He cried with those who were sad. Then he made the ultimate sacrifice of love, giving his life so we could live forever with him.

Motivated by Jesus' sacrifice and with his Holy Spirit living in us, let's pray for opportunities to share his love with others in tangible, messy ways. Let's not be afraid to get our hands dirty. That type of sacrificial love can then lead to us sharing our "why" with them.

Why do we love? **"Because** [God] **first loved us"** (1 John 4:19).

August 11

Never forgotten
Jon Enter

It was a busy morning in the emergency room. Around 8:30 A.M. an elderly gentleman in his 80s arrived to have stitches removed from his thumb. He told the nurse he was in a hurry due to an appointment at 9:15 A.M. The nurse took his vital signs and had him take a seat, knowing it would be over an hour before he was seen. The elderly man kept looking at his watch with great concern.

Given his age, the nurse moved him up the list and got him in next to be seen. After the stitches were removed, the older man thanked the nurse and tried to hurry away. Before he left, the curious nurse asked if his next appointment was another doctor's visit. "No," he replied with a smile, "I meet my wife every day at her nursing home for breakfast at 9:15 A.M. She has Alzheimer's disease." The nurse replied, "She wouldn't know if you missed just one time, right?" The man replied, "Although she has forgotten who I am, I know who she is."

That's the kind of love Christ shows you. Even though there are times you live as if you've forgotten his laws, even though there are times your excuses push him away, Jesus knows you. He loves you. He declares in Isaiah 44:21, **"I have made you. . . . I will not forget you."**

Jesus comes after you. He is never out to get back at you; he's out to get you back to him.

August 12

God remembers
Nate Wordell

Great middle school teachers have something in common with great coaches and great parents. They remember what it was like to be young: When the middle school students consist mostly of hormones, when the athletes are super nervous, when the toddler is on his third temper tantrum of the hour—then it's helpful for the adults to have a bit of compassion, to remember what it was like to be young.

I bet God would be an amazing teacher or coach because he is a great Father. If God looks across the room at you today and sees you acting on hormones or super nervous or throwing a tantrum, he remembers. He can think back to when he grabbed some dirt from the Garden of Eden and shaped it to look like you. He remembers that your origins are in dirt. He knows your limitations and, like the best dad, he has compassion on you. He remembers that he needed to do all the work to save you, and he won't let your sin stand in his way.

The Lord remembers what it is like to be made of dust because he has been there. Jesus, as a real human being, knows about crazy weeks, nerves, and tantrums, and he knows how much you need him, so he promised to be with you always.

"As a father has compassion on his children, so the Lord has compassion on those who fear him; for he knows how we are formed, he remembers that we are dust" (Psalm 103:13,14).

August 13

Be a beggar
Linda Buxa

There's an account in Mark 5 where Jesus got out of a boat in a place called the Gerasenes and a demon-possessed man who had been living in tombs came to meet him. Now, while the focus is (and should be) on Jesus setting the man free, I can't help but notice all the begging.

The demon-possessed man said, **"I beg you before God, don't torment me!"** Then **"he begged him earnestly not to send them out of the region"** (verses 7,10 CSB). Then the demons joined in and **"begged him, 'Send us to the pigs, so that we may enter them.'"** On top of that, the people in the area **"began to beg [Jesus] to leave their region"** (verses 12,17 CSB). And after Jesus healed the man, the restored man **"begged him earnestly that he might remain with him"** (verse 18 CSB).

All that begging made me realize that sometimes my prayers are a little lukewarm and not nearly earnest enough. I think I need to learn from these examples to beg more and beg boldly. I'm not begging out of shame but because I have confidence in the relationship. I know I am a dearly loved child who has the privilege of approaching a delighted Father.

There's another thing I needed to realize too. For all the begging in the Gerasenes, Jesus answered some of the begging with a yes and some of it with a no, but that didn't stop the people from being bold. They weren't afraid to ask Jesus.

August 14

The easy way and the hard way
Matt Trotter

When I was a kid, I was coached by my dad to do some things the hard way. One particular "hard way" he taught me was to bend down and make sure I hadn't missed a row of grass as I mowed our lawn. I wonder what the neighbors thought? As I aged and cut grass for money, I'd bend down and check, making sure the tallest blade of grass was cut like the rest. Bending over to check the quality of my work was the hard way.

Sharing the good news of Jesus can be hard. As a believer, the easy but ineffective way is to hold out the law: "You shall not." But as imperfect people, we are guilty of not always keeping the law. When we falter, we can become hypocrites. Yikes!

Yes, there's a place for the law in the good news because it shows us our need for Jesus. But the hard way of sharing the good news with others is admitting guilt: "This is a tempting one, brother. It tempts me too, but Jesus is with us." The apostle Paul wrote, **"For all have sinned and fall short of the glory of God, and all are justified freely by his grace through the redemption that came by Christ Jesus"** (Romans 3:23,24).

God encourages us to lead people with the light of Jesus' love and forgiveness, not with rules. Sometimes that's hard "in the moment." I think this is the hard way for two reasons: for our own hearts and to protect those watching us work across the street.

August 15

The danger of "do-it-yourself"
Jan Gompper

We live in a do-it-yourself age. On YouTube you can find videos on how to assemble your new grill, test your car's alternator, get a wine stain out of your carpet, make homemade cheese . . . I even saw a video on "how to suture like a surgeon"—ouch!

Being able to do things ourselves is great. It usually saves us money and gives us a sense of pride in our accomplishment. The do-it-yourself mindset starts early. Toddlers quickly push away their parents' hands and say, "I do it!" when trying to dress themselves or pour their own glasses of milk.

When you think about it, our do-it-yourself instincts come naturally because we were created in the image of the ultimate do-it-yourselfer—the One who created the world from *nothing*.

Unfortunately, Adam and Eve's inherent do-it-yourself instincts went awry when they thought they could do it themselves without the One who created them. **"The man and his wife . . . hid from the Lord God among the trees"** (Genesis 3:8 NLT).

We would still be hiding had our merciful God not done what only he could do himself. He sent his only Son to pay the penalty for humankind's do-it-yourself disobedience.

Now we can stand confidently before God without fear because **"we are confident of all this because of our great trust in God through Christ. It is not that we think we are qualified to do anything on our own. Our qualification comes from God"** (2 Corinthians 3:4,5 NLT).

August 16

Screen time check
Mike Novotny

"Show me your screen time," I asked a high schooler whom I mentor. He showed me his phone, which said—15 hours and 38 minutes per day! Whoa. "Ask three of your friends for their screen time," I followed up, and he did. Soon after, he came back with the data—9 hours per day, 12 and a half hours per day, and just over 13 hours per day. Whoa. Whoa. Whoa.

How about you? What's your number? Not including work or school, the average American spends 5-6 hours each day on screens. If you're under 30, the number is more like 9-11 hours/day. How do you feel about that?

While I want to be careful not to add rules where the Bible has not given them, I do want to remind you of what Moses once taught: **"[Our days] quickly pass, and we fly away"** (Psalm 90:10). While your days might seem long, your decades will fly by. Your time is limited, irreversible, and precious to God.

I won't suggest the "right" amount of screen time for someone whose life is meant to honor God and love others, but I will challenge you with this question—What do you *really* want to do this week? What *really* matters when this month is over? What are you *really* pursuing with your one and only life?

Let the Holy Spirit guide you to a noble, compelling, and regret-free answer. Then act accordingly.

August 17

Point and call
Liz Schroeder

Can pointing and calling save lives? According to Wikipedia, "Pointing and calling is a method in occupational safety for avoiding mistakes by pointing at important indicators and verbally calling out their status." But you don't have to work in a dangerous industry to use it. When you leave the house, you can point and say, "All the stove knobs are off. My phone is in my pocket."

In the Christian church, we don't necessarily say, "Point and call." We say, "Confession and absolution." But confession and absolution aren't just for Sunday morning. Consider this: **"Encourage one another *daily*, as long as it is called 'Today,' so that none of you may be hardened by sin's deceitfulness"** (Hebrews 3:13).

What if pointing out sin and calling others to repentance became as routine as making sure your appliances were off? I wonder if sins like adultery could be avoided by pointing out important indicators like not prioritizing the marriage relationship. I wonder if sins like gluttony could be avoided by pointing out a loved one's habit of using food to self-medicate. Helping a friend keep a sensitive conscience and take out the spiritual trash are ways to prevent becoming hardened by sin's deceitfulness.

What if pointing to the cross and calling out for mercy became as common as making sure you had your phone? It would be cruel to point out destructive patterns without offering a way out. That way out is the cross of Jesus. .

Whom do you love enough to use the "point and call" method today?

August 18

I'm here for Jesus
Matt Ewart

Imagine a group of prisoners standing in a circle, each one sharing why they're behind bars. One says, "I'm here for armed robbery." Another says, "I'm here for drug charges." A third says, "I'm here for financial fraud." Each person's story is a consequence of their own choices.

Then a fourth person speaks up. It's the apostle Paul. He looks around and simply says, "I'm here for Jesus."

Paul wasn't in prison because of any wrongdoing. He was in chains because of the gospel. In Philippians 1:13, Paul writes, **"As a result, it has become clear throughout the whole palace guard and to everyone else that I am in chains for Christ."**

Paul's chains weren't a punishment for something he did wrong. They were a direct result of his unwavering commitment to sharing Christ. He didn't see his imprisonment as a setback; rather, he saw it as an opportunity for the gospel to spread farther.

His "I'm here for Jesus" mindset was a response to what Jesus did for him and for you. When Jesus lived in this world, he could have said, "I'm here for me." He could have chosen the simple life or demanded glory as the Son of God. But instead, he took up the cross and said, "I'm here for you." He laid down his life to reconcile you to God.

So wherever you might find yourself today, say along with the apostle Paul, "I'm here for Jesus." Live as if he placed you *here* for a purpose. Because he did.

August 19

The Bible's most important teaching on money
Mike Novotny

A few weeks ago, I sprung a question about finances on my colleague Pastor Michael. If you don't know him, Michael is a lifelong follower of Jesus who raised six children on a meager missionary's salary and considers personal finance one of his passions. I asked that more than qualified Christian this question: "What do you think is the Bible's most important teaching on money?"

He said without pause, "It's all God's."

I couldn't agree more. Psalm 24 says, **"The earth is the Lord's, and everything in it"** (verse 1). Because God created everything, everything belongs to him. In other words, we're all in management, called to handle faithfully the dollars, days, and possessions God puts into our hands. To say it another way: What we own is God's on loan. Or, if you're a fan of *The Office*, you might say you're God's Michael Scott, a regional manager of what the Boss Upstairs owns.

Why does that matter? First, it catapults your gratitude as you realize how absurdly generous God is toward you every day. Your clothes, car, and cat all belong to God, but he loaned them in love to you. Second, it increases your responsibility to generosity, since your money is really God's money and God commands us to be generous with his money. Finally, it blesses you with peace, knowing that God is right in the middle of your financial situation, promising to care for you and give you what you truly need (Matthew 6:32).

All you own is God's on loan. Few financial truths matter more than that.

August 20

The underdog
Ann Jahns

During the 1980 Olympics, the world watched as the underdog U.S. hockey team battled the heavily favored Russian team. No one expected the Americans to win. At the final buzzer, the U.S. team held the lead as the Russians stared at the scoreboard, stunned. The game has since been dubbed the "Miracle on Ice," and it's one of the greatest triumphs in sports history.

Do you love a good underdog story? We all love to see the little guy come out on top.

On the surface, Jesus was an underdog. He was from no-name Nazareth, our version of the wrong side of the tracks. He was the son of a poor craftsman. The prophet Isaiah tells us that Jesus wasn't much to look at. He didn't have a home and traveled around with a ragtag band of friends on the fringes of polite society.

But there was more to this underdog than met the eye. Beneath his humble exterior, this average man was true God. And boy, did his enemies—among them Satan himself—underestimate him. Revelation talks about their defeat at the hands of King Jesus: **"They will wage war against the Lamb, but the Lamb will triumph over them because he is Lord of lords and King of kings— and with him will be his called, chosen and faithful followers"** (17:14).

Jesus is no underdog. He is the magnificent and all-powerful true God. Through his triumph over sin and death, we—his called, chosen, and faithful followers— are the victors as well!

August 21

Say something worth hearing
Jason Nelson

Ancient Greek playwrights used a gimmicky plot device to solve hopeless problems they wrote into their tragedies. Out of nowhere something phenomenal would appear to bring resolution to the situation. The Romans dubbed it *deus ex machina*, "god out of a machine." The practice continues today and is an expedient way to get to an ending. The cavalry arrives in the nick of time. The end. Then everyone can live happily ever after.

Pastors could start using ChatGPT to help them write their sermons. That could cut down on prep time. Those sermons might be well crafted and noticeably similar. We could start tuning them out because we know what to expect.

Since the industrial revolution, people have been afraid that machines will replace them and dehumanize our existence. Mechanical things, robotic things, and microprocessors are commonplace on the assembly line, in the operating room, and they let us do our banking at all hours. It's all been good. And we're still here.

My son-in-law is a scholar. He says, "If you can say something profound, you will always have an audience." Here is something profound: **"God is love. Whoever lives in love lives in God, and God in them"** (1 John 4:16). I'm not sure a machine could unpack that text. Machines can disseminate God's Word. But God's love only lives in people. And God's love is best expressed to others by people like you and me.

August 22

This repetition was different
C.L. Whiteside

I've probably read certain parts of Scripture over 50 times in my life, but one section spoke to me in a new and unique way this time. God's Word is designed to do this—to reveal fresh insights and remind us of who God truly is.

Sometimes we're tempted to think we don't need to read or hear a passage because we've heard it before and already know what it says. But we often forget. To fully grasp God's Word, I've found it helpful to look at the surrounding passages, reading full chapters or even entire books.

For example, I was reading about King David when he was about to have an affair with Bathsheba. I had always viewed him as lazy and arrogant in that moment. But since I had read the preceding chapters—seeing how he had spent years running for his life, enduring Saul's attacks, and fighting battle after battle—I began to understand how easy it would've been for him to desire a break and then lose focus on God.

We often don't realize that we view Scripture through different lenses depending on the season of life we're in. We often forget that God wants to speak to us through his Word. Hebrews 4:12 reminds us, **"For the word of God is alive and active. Sharper than any double-edged sword, it penetrates even to dividing soul and spirit, joints and marrow; it judges the thoughts and attitudes of the heart."**

Every repetition with God is meaningful. It's special. It's necessary. And it gives life.

August 23

Even to your old age
Nathan Nass

There's an end date to just about everything in life. Good or bad, everything ends. School ends when you're 18 or maybe 22. Friendships end when someone moves away. Sports often end after elementary school or high school. Even the best athletes have to stop by the time they're 40. Work ends at 65 or 70. There's an end date to just about everything in life. Good or bad, everything ends.

Except one thing: God's care for you. It never ends, no matter how old you get. Here's God's promise to you: **"Even to your old age and gray hairs I am he, I am he who will sustain you. I have made you and I will carry you; I will sustain you and I will rescue you"** (Isaiah 46:4). God cares for you, even to your old age! God will sustain you, even to your old age! God will carry you, even to your old age! God will rescue you, even to your old age!

As you go through life, it can seem like you're losing one thing after another. Relationships end. Loved ones die. Health gives out. Work stops. It's easy to say: "What's left? What hope do I have?"

This: "Even to your old age and gray hairs I am he." The Savior who died on a cross to forgive your sins has no plans to leave you ever. There's one thing that never ends: Jesus' love for you, even to your old age!

August 24

Jesus, lover of women
Daron Lindemann

Jesus loved women. No, he was not a womanizer. Womanizers don't love women as much as they love themselves. Jesus loved women in a pure, deep, selfless, and inspiring kind of way. He also got in trouble for it. A rabbi at that time was not supposed to speak to a woman in public (not even his own wife).

Jesus engaged the Samaritan woman at the well in conversation. When his disciples returned and saw Jesus with her, they **"were surprised to find him talking with a woman"** (John 4:27).

Jesus touched and healed Peter's mother-in-law and took by the hand Jairus' dead daughter, raising her back to life. A sick woman reached through a crowd to touch Jesus and was healed.

Jesus allowed a prostitute to wipe his feet with her hair and some expensive perfume. Jesus commended a poor widow for giving a penny to church—because it's all she had to live on. Jesus rescued a woman who, according to religious rules, deserved to be stoned to death.

Jesus benefitted from the kindness and help of some women who followed him like his disciples. Jesus treasured his friendship with Mary and Martha.

The first person to see Jesus alive after he rose from the dead was a woman, Mary Magdalene. And Jesus submitted to the parenting authority and love of a special woman, his mother.

May we, the church, the body of Christ, follow his example today. May we bless women with his love.

August 25

True Christianity offers community
Mike Novotny

Recently, I sat down with a newly married couple who has caught fire in their faith. I wish you could have been there. "We got addicted to [church]," they smiled. At first, the idea of true Christian community intimidated them—"Telling people about my life? Are you serious?"—but now they can't imagine life without it. "We have so many people we can fall back on."

King David would get that. He wrote, **"I say of the holy people who are in the land, 'They are the noble ones in whom is all my delight'"** (Psalm 16:3). David was not some lone spiritual wolf but instead delighted in the holy people in the land, the ones he did life with.

I hope you do too. You and I aren't independently spiritual people, each sharing our thoughts and feelings that originated in the human heart. No, we are Christians, pointing one another to Christ, our King, who revealed himself in the Word of God. Christian community is messy and flawed and often so very, very human. But here we meet people who love our souls, who pray for our strength, who answer our texts. We meet people who remind us of God's authority, nudging us to repentance, and they speak to us of God's safety and about the forgiveness we find in Jesus.

You could do life alone, but how much better to do life together!

August 26

Your purpose may be to raise up a leader
Matt Trotter

The Monastery of St. Andrew near Argostoli, Greece, which dates to the 13th century, claims to have quite the relic—a foot of the apostle Andrew. It's kept in a display case with a bejeweled slipper. On a recent visit, it took me a moment to realize, "Yes, that's an anklebone." But then I thought of Romans 10:15: **"How beautiful are the feet of those who bring good news!"** After John the Baptist, Andrew is the second or third person whom John records telling the good news of Jesus. Andrew shared the news about Jesus with his brother, Peter. Andrew's work was to share that news.

"Andrew, Simon Peter's brother, was one of the two who heard what John had said and who had followed Jesus. The first thing Andrew did was to find his brother Simon and tell him, 'We have found the Messiah' (that is, the Christ). And he brought him to Jesus.

"Jesus looked at him and said, 'You are Simon son of John. You will be called Cephas' (which, when translated, is Peter [meaning Rock])" (John 1:40-42).

What's the lesson for us? Sometimes it's our job to raise up the next person. Andrew's work was important and necessary, and it's hard to imagine what would have happened had he lacked the courage to share Jesus with his brother. Thankfully he did. And through Peter and the other apostles, Jesus established the New Testament church.

August 27

Pastors must not love money
Mike Novotny

One of the Bible's most famous verses on money says, **"The love of money is a root of all kinds of evil"** (1 Timothy 6:10). But do you know to whom those words were originally written? Pastors.

Timothy, to whom this letter was written, was a pastor. Also, this letter is mostly addressing those who teach others the Christian message (pastors). Finally, the idea of loving money is mentioned earlier in this same letter in Paul's list of qualifications for being a pastor: **"The overseer [pastor] is to be . . . not a lover of money"** (1 Timothy 3:2,3). Why talk so much about pastors and money? Because a money-loving pastor is a root of all kinds of evil.

A pastor who loves what God's people give more than God's people themselves is a church wrecking ball. When his motives are discovered, he will smash people's trust in the church and disconnect entire families from the gospel message for years, if not generations. His greed will stunt people's giving, which will sabotage the church's ability to carry out Jesus' mission to make more disciples. This is why God came in swift judgment when Ananias and Sapphira's greed crept into the early Christian church (read more in Acts 5:1-11). This is why he still cares about pastors' hearts today.

The next time you pray the Lord's Prayer, think of your pastor and all pastors: "Our Father, lead us not into temptation. Deliver us from evil." *Father, may every pastor be content, void of greed, and eager to give instead of get. In Jesus' name. Amen!*

August 28

The Lord is near
Nathan Nass

The Lord is near. It often doesn't feel that way, does it? Heaven seems far away. God seems far away. Help and hope seem far away. At least, that's what the devil wants you to believe.

But the Lord is near. He is near to you. Here's the Bible's promise: **"The Lord is near to all who call on him, to all who call on him in truth"** (Psalm 145:18). The Lord is not far away. The Lord is near to every single person who calls on him in truth. Wouldn't it be great to have God always right there with you?

So how can you call on him in truth? Only through Jesus. Jesus told his disciples: **"I am the way and the truth and the life. No one comes to the Father except through me"** (John 14:6). When Jesus died for you on a cross, he opened up the way to God the Father. Jesus is the way! Every believer in Jesus can call out to God through Jesus—the Way, the Truth, and the Life.

The Lord is near. The Lord is near to you. When you sin, don't turn away from God. Call out to him through Jesus, your Savior. When you feel all alone, don't despair. Call out to the Lord and listen for his voice in the Word. When you struggle to face life's struggles, don't be afraid. Call on the Lord. The Lord is near to you.

August 29

God really, really loves you
Dave Scharf

"You like me! You really, really like me!" Do you remember who said that? It was Sally Field in an Oscar acceptance speech about how badly she wanted the respect of her peers. Deep down, we can all relate to wanting to win the approval of peers. Even more important though is winning God's approval. Look at your life. I don't think I need to convince you. You and I can't do it. We deserve God's anger, not his approval.

But the psalmist says, **"You forgave the iniquity of your people and covered all their sins. I will listen to what God the Lord says; he promises peace to his people, his faithful servants"** (85:2,8).

God gives us peace in forgiveness. How? By sending a package shipped from heaven, wrapped in rags, and arriving just in time for Christmas. The package marked "Peace" weighed no more than ten pounds and fit in the nook of a mother's arm. God gave peace, not because his heart melted at the cuteness of Jesus. God did not simply overlook our sins. He forgave them by turning his anger from us onto his only Son, who was on a cross. And having wiped every sin away from us, he smiled on us and gave us the peace that Jesus won.

God looks at you and is pleased. Carry around that peace today, and reflect your Savior's love to everyone you meet. Why? Because God loves you. He really, really loves you.

August 30

No alternative
Matt Ewart

How can God love someone like me?

Usually people don't vocalize that question to me, but I can hear it hidden behind their guilt-filled confessions. I can see doubt in God's love in the tired eyes of those who have been chained by addiction. I sense a questioning of God's love when people in their retirement years share their regrets, revealing the burned bridges they've left behind. Truth be told, I sometimes ask myself this question when I reflect on things I didn't get right or things I could have done better.

How can God love someone like me?

What we all need to hear is that God does love us. And what we all need to understand is why he does. I am absolutely confident that God loves both me and you for one specific reason: Jesus took care of the alternative.

When Jesus died on a cross, he took away the alternative for us—eternal separation from God. Through his sacrifice, Jesus absorbed the punishment for our sin. The weight of our failure, the cost of our guilt, and the consequences of our wrongs were all placed on him. Jesus faced what we deserved.

Because of this, God's love is no longer a "maybe." It's not something we can question. It is a guarantee, because **"all are justified freely by his grace through the redemption that came by Christ Jesus"** (Romans 3:24).

Today, rest in the certainty that because Jesus endured the alternative, grace is guaranteed for you.

August 31

The God you can see or hear
C.L. Whiteside

A guy named Ken once told a story about how he was short on rent and facing eviction. He considered skipping church to do odd jobs but had already committed to attending church. He prayed about his situation, went to church, and—unexpectedly—an older woman walked up to him and handed him an envelope with $1,000 inside, the exact amount he needed for rent. Amazing, right?!

If you don't think you've ever experienced a miraculous intervention in your life, that's okay. Sometimes we question if something is wrong with us or even wonder if God loves us when we compare our experiences to what other Christians say they feel, hear, or see. But while God can work in such ways, he's not limited to them.

And when someone says, "God told me to do this!" it's not always truly from him. If you hear a voice or feel a nudge, remember God will never contradict what he has already said in his Word. Wanting to hear or feel God's presence is natural, but realize he primarily speaks to us through his Word. Hebrews 4:12 reminds us that Scripture not only speaks to us but also exposes our innermost thoughts and desires.

Too often, we forget to take time to listen to God. We rush through life without pausing to pray, meditate, or be still in his presence. Psalm 46:10 gives us a simple yet powerful reminder: **"Be still, and know that I am God."** Make it a priority to spend time each day quieting your heart and truly listening to his Word.

SEPTEMBER

Each of you should use whatever gift you have received to serve others, as faithful stewards of God's grace in its various forms.

1 PETER 4:10

September 1

Eating too much?
Mike Novotny

I meandered around the church office asking my coworkers, "On a scale of 0 to 100, how much of a glutton are you?" (Yes, I actually do things like this.) There were instant grimaces, thoughtful pauses, and clarifying questions such as, "What exactly is gluttony?"

Gluttony is a taboo topic that many Christians avoid, but it's one that deserves our attention. It isn't essentially about our size, shape, or weight but rather about how the quantity of our food affects the quality of our faith.

The words *glutton* and *gluttony* appear seven times in Scripture, which I would like to share with you in a series of devotions. To begin, here's the word's first appearance, where some out-of-ideas parents bring their prodigal son to the elders of Israel: **"They** [the parents] **shall say to the elders, 'This son of ours is stubborn and rebellious. He will not obey us. He is a glutton and a drunkard'"** (Deuteronomy 21:20). Notice how an excess of food (glutton) is combined with an excess of alcohol (drunkard), a combo that shows up in a majority of the seven Bible references to gluttony.

Why is too much food such an issue? I'll explain more in our upcoming devotions, but here's the heart of it: When you eat too much, you love too little. Overindulgence in food means you will, due to a lack of energy, underserve your neighbor in love.

Let's ponder our personal relationships with food and ask God to balance our portion size so we can maximize our love.

September 2

Too much food = drowsiness
Mike Novotny

When you eat too much, you love too little. After studying all seven references to gluttony in the Bible, this is the conclusion that I came to, a conclusion that I needed since I LOVE food.

Here's the primary Scripture that led me to that conclusion: **"Listen, my son, and be wise, and set your heart on the right path: Do not join those who drink too much wine or gorge themselves on meat, for drunkards and gluttons become poor, and drowsiness clothes them in rags"** (Proverbs 23:19-21). Eating too much food or drinking too much wine leads to "drowsiness," among other things.

I bet you already knew that. It's most obvious an hour after a Thanksgiving feast, but you've felt that drowsiness after any supersized meal. God designed your body for a certain amount of food, and when you violate that design, a consequence is drowsiness.

Why does that matter? Because an hour after your meal, God has good works for you to do. God has, perhaps, a good book he wanted you to learn from, a time of prayer he wanted you to be alert during, a spouse he wanted you to listen to, a neighbor who needed a hand with a home project, or a kid who needed more than another day with Dad zoned out on his phone. But you can't pour much love into them if you've just put too much food into you.

Why is God against gluttony? Because God is for love.

September 3

Eat to love
Mike Novotny

If I gave you an essay question that read, "Why did God create food?," what would you write?

Personally, I would put down two answers. First, God made food for your pleasure. When he knit you together in your mother's womb, he crafted a body that would end up with thousands of taste buds to sense the sweet, the salty, the savory, and more. Human fuel could be a thick, gray, tasteless paste, but it isn't. It's a crisp tortilla chip, a perfectly grilled steak, a vine-ripened tomato because God made food for your pleasure. (Can I get an Amen?!)

Second, God made food for his purpose—to fuel your body to love others. Without food, you lack the calories needed to get up, lend a hand, think deeply about a problem, play on the carpet with your kid, help a friend move a sleeper sofa (the true proof of friendship!), write a Christ-centered sermon, or balance the family finances.

This is why God cares about gluttony. When you and I get too excited about the pleasure, we undo the purpose. When I pound three donuts in the break room because I crave the pleasure, I end up sluggish, weary, and can't fulfill the purpose.

God isn't against good food. You can love to eat. Just make sure you eat to love. **"So whether you eat or drink or whatever you do, do it all for the glory of God"** (1 Corinthians 10:31).

September 4

Honor God in all you do
Mike Novotny

When I studied the Bible's seven passages on gluttony, I was confronted and comforted. The confrontation happened when I realized that too much food leads to too little love, that overdoing the pleasure of a heaping portion undermines the purpose of fueling up to serve my neighbor.

But the comfort was in how close Jesus got to people like me. In accusing Jesus of sin, his enemies claimed, **"Here is a glutton and a drunkard, a friend of tax collectors and sinners"** (Luke 7:34). The first part was a lie, of course, since Jesus lived a sinless live of perfect self-control. He ate but never was a glutton. He drank but never was a drunkard. The second part, however, was gloriously true. Jesus was the friend of sinners. He didn't keep his distance from drunks and gluttons, from tax collectors and sinners. Instead, he drew near to them, loved them, called them to repentance, and offered them forgiveness.

Jesus does the same for you and me. Instead of staying far from us, Jesus drew near, leaving heaven and coming to our Earth. His Word confronts our infatuation with short-term, sinful pleasure. His death on a cross is the answer for our drunkenness and gluttony, for our sins of the mind and of the mouth. His resurrection is the proof that our debt has been paid and he is eternally alive and well to help us in our time of need.

Nothing makes us want to honor God in all we do, including eating our next meal, quite like the love of Jesus!

September 5

Back to school tears
Daron Lindemann

It's an exciting day! First day of school! Complete with some tears, especially in preschool families. Why? There's little to be afraid of. School is a safe, friendly place that's oozing with a teacher's love, colorful toys, Smart Boards, and frosted cupcakes. So why the tears?

Because the closeness and intimacy of a family's love is being tested. Preschoolers wonder, "Are Mom and Dad leaving me forever?" Mom and Dad wonder, "Will our preschooler grow up in seven hours, graduate, move to Spain, and be gone from our lives?"

What will happen to your family's love, Mom and Dad, as you leave your child at a Christian school? It will grow bigger and get stronger. How? The love of God. You are leaving your child—momentarily away from your presence—in the presence of God their Father.

One mom in the Bible experienced this. Her name was Hannah. She took her son Samuel to the church school and left him there. Hannah knew that Samuel's love for God needed to develop without the interference of her own uncertainties.

Hannah recalls, **"'I prayed for this child, and the Lord has granted me what I asked of him. So now I give [Samuel] to the Lord. For his whole life he will be given over to the Lord.' And he worshiped the Lord there"** (1 Samuel 1:27,28).

When Hannah dropped off Samuel, he may have shed a tear, but it gave way to something he knew and loved even more than his mom. His God.

September 6

Gloating season
Liz Schroeder

There is a long gloating season in Phoenix. Phoenicians tend to brag about their nine glorious months of sunny, temperate weather while our family and friends in other parts of the country scrape ice off of car windshields and wear parkas over their Halloween costumes. Anyone who visits us in July, August, or September, however, must be crazy or really love us, because it's miserable. And don't give me that "But it's a dry heat!" garbage. You know what else is a dry heat? A pizza oven. I don't want to live in one of those. We are all ready for summer to be over and for gloating season to return.

Jesus must be crazy or really love us to come to this planet. Why would someone leave the perfection of heaven to make himself nothing? Philippians 2 says that **"he humbled himself by becoming obedient to death—even death on a cross!"** (verse 8). Jesus set aside his glory to endure the cross so we can enjoy heaven for eternity.

"Therefore God exalted him to the highest place and gave him the name that is above every name, that at the name of Jesus every knee should bow, in heaven and on earth and under the earth, and every tongue acknowledge that Jesus Christ is Lord, to the glory of God the Father" (verses 9-11).

If you yearn for the season you are in to end and ache for wrongs to be made right, remember that Christ is preparing a perfect, temperature-controlled mansion for you in heaven.

September 7

Set aside the old ways
Matt Trotter

When you're a new Christian, one of the harder Bible concepts to understand is a new covenant. A covenant is a contract. The Bible is divided into two covenant parts, the Old Testament and the New Testament. The old contract and the new contract. The Old Testament was established in word by the work of Moses, and it's now set aside for a new covenant with Jesus (the New Testament).

In the Old Testament, God defined living according to his laws. Yet so much of the old laws were set aside by Christ in the new covenant, the gospel, which in Greek means "good news."

God tells of this day already in the Old Testament book of Jeremiah: **"'No longer will they teach their neighbor, or say to one another, "Know the Lord," because they will all know me, from the least of them to the greatest,' declares the Lord. 'For I will forgive their wickedness and will remember their sins no more'"** (31:34).

The writer of the New Testament book Hebrews cites Jeremiah and ends with this mighty punctuation mark: **"By calling this covenant 'new,' he has made the first one obsolete; and what is obsolete and outdated will soon disappear"** (Hebrews 8:13).

Everything is different because of Jesus. So now, Jesus gets it all. Jesus gets all of our souls, all of our time, all of our money, all of our priorities. No matter where we are, we live not in fear of the old contract but in celebration of the good news of Jesus!

September 8

The Lord is your light
Nathan Nass

"How could there be light before there was the sun?" I hear people ask that. If you know the Bible's creation story, you've heard that God created the world in six days. On the first day, God said, **"Let there be light"** (Genesis 1:3), and there was light. Yet God didn't make the sun until the fourth day of creation. How could there be light before there was the sun?

Because the Lord is our light. Later in the Bible, as God described the salvation he would bring to his people, he told them, **"The sun will no more be your light by day, nor will the brightness of the moon shine on you, for the Lord will be your everlasting light, and your God will be your glory"** (Isaiah 60:19). In heaven, there is no sun. Why? The Lord is our light! Even here on earth, light in our lives doesn't depend on whether the sun is shining. Why? "The Lord will be your everlasting light."

Is your life darkened by guilt? Jesus died on a cross to take your sins away. The Lord is your light! Is your life clouded by loneliness? Jesus is with you everywhere every day. The Lord is your light! Do you feel hopeless? Jesus promises eternal life in heaven to all who believe in him. The Lord is your light!

Light in your life doesn't depend on the sun. It depends on Jesus. The Lord is your light!

September 9

Eyes of faith
Linda Buxa

On December 21, 2020, there was a "great conjunction" of Jupiter and Saturn. On that day, Jupiter and Saturn appeared closer in Earth's night sky than they had for 397 years. But as meteorological luck would have it, it was cloudy that night, and I never got to see it.

It reminded me of the time my family visited Mount St. Helens in 2013. It was so foggy that we couldn't even see past the visitor lookout. In both cases, we knew the planets and mountain were there. We saw reports on the news, and our friends shared photos. And I've been to Mount St. Helens multiple times (before and after the eruption).

What a good reminder about my faith. I can't see Jesus with my eyes right now, but people who did see him wrote books about him, leaving written proof.

Was I hoping to see the conjunction? Yep. But that didn't happen, and I won't be here in 800 years for the next one. That's okay. I've learned to live with disappointment in the temporary.

Am I hoping to see Jesus? Yep. And this one *will* happen; I just don't know when. I've learned to live with joyful hope and yearning for the eternal.

"Though you have not seen him, you love him; and even though you do not see him now, you believe in him and are filled with an inexpressible and glorious joy, for you are receiving the end result of your faith, the salvation of your souls" (1 Peter 1:8,9).

September 10

Never be comfortable with this
C.L. Whiteside

Sometimes I see something on social media or the news and am amazed at how much wickedness there is. Some things our culture agrees are egregious while others are dismissed as "to each his own" and not seen as wicked. Yet sin is what tears families apart, wrecks unity, shatters dreams, and ruins individuals' psyches. The spouse who inflicted deep wounds on their family, the person publicly humiliated, the man who lost his freedom, and the woman trapped in a cycle of shameful acts—chances are, it all started with a sin they thought wasn't too bad.

Don't be comfortable with any sin. God is so serious about sin that he says in Matthew 5:29, **"If your right eye causes you to stumble, gouge it out and throw it away."** So how do we avoid spiritual pitfalls?

First, we turn to God's Word to understand truly what is right and wrong. In our culture, what's wrong today may not be wrong tomorrow, but with God's Word, truth remains clear and unchanging. The law of God in the Bible serves as a curb, mirror, and guide for us.

Second, we must not shy away from the fact that God hates sin. Instead, we embrace that truth—because while God hates sin, he also loves us so much that he left heaven, lived a perfect life as a human, suffered an undeserved death on a cross, paid a debt we couldn't pay, and gave us the freedom no longer to be slaves to sin.

Jesus wasn't comfortable with sin—and thankfully, it doesn't have to control or define believers.

September 11

Seeking God's glory
Nathan Nass

Whose glory are you seeking today? Whom do you want to make look good? Whom do you want people to praise? Whom do you want to draw attention to? Each day, you and I are seeking glory for someone.

If we're honest, usually that person is you or me. How many of our words and actions cry out, "Look at me! Look at what I can do! Praise me!"

Jesus has some convicting words for us. It's like a little test for our hearts. He once said, **"Whoever speaks on their own does so to gain personal glory, but he who seeks the glory of the one who sent him is a man of truth"** (John 7:18). How do you know if someone is a man or woman of truth? That person seeks God's glory. That person yearns for God to be praised. That person's life is like a billboard pointing to Jesus: "Look at him! Look at what he's done! Praise Jesus!"

Do you know who empowers us to seek Jesus' glory? Jesus does! Jesus looks at you all the time. Jesus loves every little act of faith you do. Jesus forgives every sin you commit. Jesus treasures you like a father treasures his child. Jesus wants only the best for you like a mother for her child.

When you realize how highly Jesus thinks of you, you never have to seek glory for yourself again. Instead, you can seek the glory of the One who died for you.

September 12

Your ways not mine
Jon Enter

Life is messy. It's painful. It often doesn't make sense.

When life goes sideways, we often wonder, "Why, God? Why would you allow THIS to happen?" There are two passages of Scripture and an illustration that give comfort. Here's the first biblical truth: **"'My thoughts are not your thoughts, neither are your ways my ways,'** **declares the Lord"** (Isaiah 55:8). Sometimes the answer to why something happens is beyond understanding. It might not even be a lesson or a teaching moment for you. It might be the opportunity for someone else to grow in their trust of God through you. But there's a purpose. That purpose is always for good. It's to bless you or others. **"We know that in all things God works for the good of those who love him, who have been called according to his purpose"** (Romans 8:28).

Even when life looks messed up, God can bring blessings and understanding. Keep your mind focused on Christ. The next sentence is a mess, but see if you can read it. Cna yuo raed tihs? I cdnuolt blveiee taht I cluod aulaclty uesdnatnrd waht I was rdanieg. Even though the letters are messed up, you are able to read it as long as the first and last letters of each word are in the right place.

Your days on earth will be messed up. Sin is here, but so is God. Start your day and end your day with trust that no matter what happens, God is in control. When you do, you will find peace.

September 13

Where is my miracle?
Jason Nelson

I have some survivor's guilt over being within a whisper of death and then recovering. I know for a fact that while I was critically ill, some very good women who were praying for me lost their husbands to sudden illness. Where was their miracle? I know for a fact that a former student who prayed for me lost her life in a tragic car accident. Where was her miracle? I feel so bad about it all. I can't wrap my mind around why I survived and others didn't. It is an existential dilemma for me.

Some well-meaning folks have suggested that I lived because God still has important things for me to do. A few have gone so far as to suggest what those might be. I'm flattered, but most days I'm not in the mood for any kind of heroics. I think we wander into a spiritual wilderness when we try to rationalize the unthinkable. Sometimes we can discern God's intentions. And sometimes he hides his face from us. But he always makes himself available to us: **"Call to me and I will answer you and tell you great and unsearchable things you do not know"** (Jeremiah 33:3). We call to him. And what finally happens could be the only clue we ever get about unsearchable things.

I'm grateful to be alive. Thank you all for praying for me. And to all of you who didn't get your miracle, I am deeply sorry for your loss.

September 14

Your will be done
Matt Ewart

When Jesus taught his disciples to pray, he told them to say, **"Your will be done"** (Matthew 6:10). Here's a prayer that will challenge you to yield to God's will today:

Dear Father in heaven, your will be done.

I pray for healing for myself and others, unless sickness is what keeps me near to you.

I pray for wisdom so that I know what to do, unless my simple understanding will serve you best.

I pray for peace in my life and throughout the world, unless conflict would draw more people to you.

I pray for plenty of daily provisions, unless poverty helps keep my hands raised to you.

I pray for your clear guidance and direction in my life, unless your silence makes me long for you.

I pray for strength to face the challenges of today, unless my weakness drives me to find strength in you.

I pray that I am filled with joy, unless sorrow or grief would deepen my dependence on you.

Lastly, Father, I pray for your forgiveness because I know it was your will to provide it through Jesus Christ, your Son, my Lord. Amen.

September 15

True grit
Jan Gompper

If you've seen the movie *True Grit*, you know it's about a young girl (Mattie Ross) who is determined to bring the man who killed her father to justice. She eventually gets connected with a bounty hunter (Rooster Cogburn) who is touted to be the toughest in the region, only to find him a drunken mess. Believing he is her only hope, she hires him anyway, trusting he has the grit (courage, resolve, strength of character) to do the job. Ironically, he learns what true grit is from her.

Have you ever been so determined to stick with or accomplish something that no obstacle could deter you? Maybe it's the 5K run you want to prove to yourself you can finish. Perhaps it's the difficult marriage you are determined not to give up on. Or is it the wayward child you will never stop praying for? All these are examples of grit.

But true grit goes further. Mattie Ross was willing to risk her very life to get justice for her father. She ended up losing a leg in the process.

The Bible speaks about true grit: **"Greater love has no one than this: to lay down one's life for one's friends"** (John 15:13). Firefighters, police officers, and soldiers come to mind.

Our grit would likely waver, however, if it meant having to die for our enemies. Yet **"while we were God's enemies, we were reconciled to him through the death of his Son"** (Romans 5:10).

That's *true* grit . . . and true love!

September 16

Jealous for Jesus
Daron Lindemann

When I think of jealousy, my mind returns to dating my girlfriend in high school. Immature infatuation. Now that I'm married to her and we have grandchildren, I don't see myself as jealous about much of anything. But I am. Are you?

King Saul burned with anger because young David killed Goliath and received more recognition for defeating enemies than Saul did. **"'They have credited David with tens of thousands,' he thought, 'but me with only thousands'"** (1 Samuel 18:8). God eventually replaced Saul with David as king of Israel because Saul saw the kingdom as his own. David saw it as God's kingdom.

We hear David's faith in his courage that faced Goliath **"in the name of the Lord Almighty"** (1 Samuel 17:45). We sing it with David in his psalms exalting God, not his own self-designed kingdom.

When you believe that God, not you, is the center of your world, it curbs sinful jealousy. David burned, not with jealousy of Saul but with jealousy for God, for Jesus, for the kingdom of God.

Be jealous for Jesus more than you are jealous of others. Desire to love Jesus more today than yesterday. Want more of Jesus.

Then, here's how you'll live. When others get good things more than you, you won't complain. When others are blessed by God in ways you aren't, it won't make you discontent. When others get to do what you want to do, it won't threaten you because you know the King loves you.

september 17

Joy is fruit
Nate Wordell

Some days I wish the Bible said, "Joy is the chocolate chip cookies of the Spirit." Then I could mix up joy like a recipe: Use one part exhilaration, two parts romance, a dash of physical fitness, and top with sugar. Bake for 12 minutes and voilá! A joyful heart created as quickly as my favorite cookies. But the Bible doesn't say that joy comes from a recipe or an assembly line or anything quite that quick and easy.

The Bible says that joy comes from farming. If a farmer wants fruit, he does a lot of things that don't look like they lead to fruit. He digs in the dirt, buries a little seed, waters the soil, pulls up weeds, aerates, fertilizes, and waits. If a farmer does all he can do, he still has to wait for God to do what only God can do. But year after year since the creation of the world, lots of hard work and supernatural blessing have led to harvest after harvest of fruit.

The Holy Spirit is a joy farmer, and he'd love to have you as a farmhand. But be warned: Sometimes cultivating joy involves a lot of things that don't look like they lead to fruit. You yank out some sin that chokes out life, dig into God's Word, pollinate with some other folks who love the Spirit, and in God's time, with God's help, you will certainly reap a harvest.

"The fruit of the Spirit is love, joy, peace, forbearance, kindness, goodness, faithfulness, gentleness and self-control" (Galatians 5:22,23).

September 18

Celebrate and be glad!
Dave Scharf

The parable of the lost son is familiar, but it's not over when the younger son returns. There are two sons. The older son is upset with the father's love for his brother. The father responds, **"My son . . . you are always with me, and everything I have is yours. But we had to celebrate and be glad, because this brother of *yours* was dead and is alive again; he was lost and is found"** (Luke 15:31,32). Jesus contrasts the younger son's restless heart and the older son's stone heart with the father's heart of grace.

Jesus shows you *his* Father in this parable, a Father so loving he was willing to let his own Son die to give you life. A Father so faithful he promises to never forget you no matter how far you wander. A Father so joyful that he's not concerned about past sins but about holding you in his arms!

So how does it end? Does the older son celebrate? It doesn't matter. What matters is this: Will you? God wants you to see yourself in *both* sons and the father's love for *both*. Then act like the father. Love with forgiveness that doesn't ask for anything in return. Love with a love willing to go out after the lost sons and daughters in your life. Love with a love that is always celebrating with the angels over *everyone* who repents. Come, let's have a feast and celebrate!

September 19

Slander and friendships?
Mike Novotny

Why do so many schools (even Christian ones) have so many problems with bullying? Why do many kids, online and in real life, pick on their classmates, making cruel jokes about their looks, their weight, and everything else? Why is slander so tempting even to the grown-up sons and daughters of God?

Because—this is sad to admit—it bonds us. When "we" have an inside joke about her, when "we" repeat that rumor about them, when "we" speculate about what he is probably like at home, those words bond us. The wink, the nod, the knowing look, being on the inside with the cool kids (even if you're fully grown) is a powerful temptation.

In middle school, in middle age, and in all the years that follow, words bond people together, but please fight the temptation to bond over the kind of words you would never want spoken about you. Many of you have a gift to connect people via your way with words. Let's pray that only happens God's way.

"Get rid of all bitterness, rage and anger, brawling and slander, along with every form of malice. Be kind and compassionate to one another, forgiving each other, just as in Christ God forgave you" (Ephesians 4:31,32). Why do we fight the temptation to slander? Why put in the hard work to be kind? Because in Christ, God has been so kind to us.

Slander slays unity and peace. Kindness repairs and restores relationships. May God help you resist the former and embrace the latter!

September 20

Hope for the future
Jon Enter

What do you hope will happen in the next few months?

Hope is an interesting word. It means different things in different contexts. Hope often means uncertainty. If you hope your football team wins the Super Bowl, that's uncertain. If you hope you'll do well on a math test without studying, that's really uncertain. But in the Bible, the word *hope* is different. When hope is connected to Christ, well, then it's rock-solid certain!

"Let us hold unswervingly to the hope we profess, for he who promised is faithful" (Hebrews 10:23). The intentional wording by the author to the Hebrew people is perfect. There is no reason to swerve to the right or the left no matter what problem is in front of you because God is with you. He's almighty. He's all-knowing. He's in the business of making the impossible possible by turning even what's bad into good. Why? He promised: **"In all things God works for the good of those who love him, who have been called according to his purpose"** (Romans 8:28). And if God promises something, he faithfully, fully fulfills his Word.

God's version of "good" might not be your version though. What you hope will happen in the next few months might not turn out as you would've written. But when the God of grace guides the novel that is your life, it's worth turning every page and living every day with an eagerness to see what God is planning next. Here's the great news: What's "good" to God is actually great!

September 21

One of the oldest prophecies about Jesus
Mike Novotny

One of the earlier and most frequently quoted prophecies about Jesus is one you need as you think about your own mortality.

Around 1,000 B.C., King David wrote, **"Therefore my heart is glad and my tongue rejoices; my body also will rest secure, because you will not abandon me to the realm of the dead, nor will you let your faithful one see decay"** (Psalm 16:9,10). Why was David so happy? Because he believed that death would not get the last word. Not when he died. And not when God's "faithful one" breathed his last.

If you've read the New Testament, you know that there's an Easter egg in David's words, a promise that 1,000 years later the apostles of Jesus would repeat. "Nor will you let *your faithful one* see decay." Did David's body decay? Yes, it did. Did David's friends die and turn into bones in their tombs? Yes, they did. So who was David talking about? He was talking about Jesus. Jesus was the truly "faithful one" who didn't decay in the grave. He rose on the third day, proving himself to be the living Lord, the conquering King, the only One worthy of your worship. That's why David was dancing and singing. His Savior offered him what no other spirituality could—happiness that has no end.

You can dance like David today too. Because Jesus didn't decay, death can't hold you down. Your last breath will be your first moment to see the face of your Savior and Lord!

September 22

Nevertheless
Nate Wordell

Nevertheless might be the greatest coordinating conjunction in history. When *nevertheless* is hooking up phrases and clauses, some unexpected change is coming.

Joseph from the Bible understood that. His brothers sold him into slavery; nevertheless, he remained faithful to God. He was falsely imprisoned; nevertheless, he served his fellow prisoners. They forgot him; nevertheless, God remembered him and made second-in-command in Egypt.

Jesus understood it too. He only loved people; nevertheless, his countrymen sentenced him to death. He kept every one of his Father's laws; nevertheless, he was abandoned on a cross for the world's sins. He died for our sins; nevertheless, he rose and reigns at God's right hand.

Jesus experienced so many painful "nevertheless" moments, and that's why Joseph had so many beautiful moments in his life and why he stuck with God.

God is still nevertheless-ing now. A mom is deprived of sleep but not of Jesus when she watches a bowl of cereal dive-bomb off the high chair and sighs, "Nevertheless."

The high school student hurries to check the posted list to see if he made the cut. He didn't, but he knows God has a "nevertheless."

A woman was looking forward to her date until it went horribly wrong. Back home she prays to a God who specializes in "nevertheless."

This day certainly has some trouble, and that's why our God came up with "nevertheless." Jesus said, **"In this world you will have trouble. But** [nevertheless] **take heart! I have overcome the world"** (John 16:33).

September 23

Mark as redeemed
Matt Ewart

One of my sons wanted to celebrate his birthday at a local arcade with some friends. We found a fantastic discount online through a third party. It saved us a lot of money, and the boys had a blast.

A month later, I received an email reminding me to redeem the credits we'd already used. When I clicked the link, I was given two options: "Redeem Now" or "Mark as Redeemed." The third party didn't know we had already used the credits, so I clicked "Mark as Redeemed" to notify them that the transaction was complete.

Today, you might need to notify someone that the transaction for your sins is complete. The accuser might unleash his attacks. Your own heart might feel burdened with guilt or regret. Pride might distract you from the payment that has already been offered on your behalf. It's good to begin every day remembering you are "marked as redeemed."

When in doubt about where you stand, remember what God says: **"And you also were included in Christ when you heard the message of truth, the gospel of your salvation. When you believed, you were marked in him with a seal, the promised Holy Spirit, who is a deposit guaranteeing our inheritance until the redemption of those who are God's possession—to the praise of his glory"** (Ephesians 1:13,14).

Stand firm in the truth of your redemption. In Christ, you are *marked as redeemed.*

September 24

Don't miss your King's glory
Dave Scharf

Do you ever miss seeing Jesus' glory because things don't look glorious? Today, you likely need to go to work or school, care for your family, do your chores, and go to bed—nothing too glorious here. King David encourages you not to miss Jesus' glory today! **"Lift up your heads, you gates . . . that the King of glory may come in. Who is he, this King of glory? The Lord Almighty—he is the King of glory"** (Psalm 24:9,10).

Missing Jesus' glory is not a new phenomenon. How many people missed the glory of the stable where he was born? I doubt the innkeeper saw the "Lord Almighty" coming to share space with the cattle in his barn. He probably just saw another peasant kid born to peasant parents. The religious leaders plotted to kill Jesus, the townspeople of his hometown of Nazareth tried to push him off a cliff, and even his disciples didn't see the glory so often. It's hard to see the breath draining from Jesus' body as he hung from a cross as glorious.

But here's the glory of it. Jesus removed your sins with his life and death. Now his glory fills your life! Jesus listens to your prayers. You have the King's ear! The King's glory is on display when you realize you live in his peace, joy, and the hope of heaven every day of this seemingly mundane life. Lift up your head, and don't miss your King's glory today!

September 25

He meets us with mercy
Linda Buxa

About 3,500 years ago, God called Moses to lead the people of Israel out of slavery in Egypt. As the people were traveling in the desert, God told Moses to build a portable worship facility called the tabernacle. God provided specific instructions about the tabernacle and its contents, including the ark of the covenant. When it came to the lid of the ark, the instructions were to **"set the mercy seat on top of the ark and put the tablets of the testimony that I will give you into the ark. I will meet with you there above the mercy seat, between the two cherubim that are over the ark of the testimony; I will speak with you from there about all that I command you regarding the Israelites"** (Exodus 25:21,22 CSB).

Isn't that amazing? God could have called that lid the "judgment seat" or "holy seat" or "perfection seat." Instead, he chose to place his presence above the "mercy seat." The God who lives in holy and inapproachable light chose to meet Moses at a place of mercy.

I guess I shouldn't be so amazed. After all, when Jesus, who was holy, took on our sin and died in our place, the cross became a mercy seat too. God chose to meet us where we did not get the punishment we deserved.

In our amazement, we say, **"Who is a God like you, who pardons sin and forgives the transgression of the remnant of his inheritance? You do not stay angry forever but delight to show mercy"** (Micah 7:18).

September 26

It changes everything
Jon Enter

"**If Christ has not been raised, your faith is futile; you are still in your sins**" (1 Corinthians 15:17). The resurrection of Jesus changes everything! The government and religious leaders wanted Jesus dead. They guarded the tomb so no one could fake him conquering death. Yet Jesus rose!

One of the greatest articles of peace a Christian has is the proof of the resurrection. Angels announced he was alive. The disciples touched his hands and side. Over 500 people saw the risen Christ, and seeing Jesus alive brought them soul-calming peace.

Charles Colson didn't believe in the resurrection until his involvement in the Watergate scandal with President Nixon became public knowledge. Charles was a professed unbeliever until he studied the resurrection, and then he said this: "I know the Resurrection is a fact, and Watergate proved it to me. How? Because 12 men testified they had seen Jesus raised from the dead, and then they proclaimed that truth for 40 years, never once denying it. Everyone was beaten, tortured, stoned, and put in prison. They would not have endured that if it weren't true. Watergate embroiled 12 of the most powerful men in the world and they couldn't keep a lie for three weeks. You're telling me 12 apostles could keep a lie for 40 years? Absolutely impossible."*

Charles came to realize that he already knew what gave him peace. Jesus is risen. Our sins are forgiven. Alleluia!

* Marty Angelo, "How Chuck Colson's Legacy of Hope Lives On," Prison Fellowship, https://www.prisonfellowship.org/2018/04/chuck-colsons-legacy-hope-lives/.

September 27

You're a peacemaker
Matt Ewart

There are two ways to experience peace in your life: Keep it, or make it.

Keeping the peace is easy. Just keep quiet. Keep to yourself. If you do have to go out and talk to people, keep things shallow. Don't rock the boat. But while avoiding conflict might feel like peace in the moment, it doesn't lead to the deep, lasting peace God desires for us. Because real peace isn't something you *keep*. It's something you *make*.

Jesus said, **"Blessed are the peacemakers, for they will be called children of God"** (Matthew 5:9).

Peacemaking is active. It requires stepping into difficult conversations with grace and humility, seeking reconciliation when it would be easier to walk away, and putting others before yourself even when it costs you. It means choosing love over resentment, understanding over assumption, and truth over silence.

But genuine peace doesn't come through force. It comes through sacrifice. Jesus himself showed us this. He didn't make peace by avoiding our sin. He made peace by confronting it with love and laying down his life to bring us back to God.

When you work for peace with the same heart, the world will take notice. They'll see something different in you. They'll recognize it as a reflection of who you are—a child of God.

So today, don't settle for keeping the peace. Be bold enough to *make* it.

September 28

Is America in a generosity crisis?
Mike Novotny

According to many voices in the world of charity and generous giving, America is in trouble. Why? Because less people are giving and people are giving less. Despite a significant increase in the total number of American households, there has been a significant decrease in the total number of households who give anything to charity. And the average American now gives less than the average American gave during the Great Depression! (That is greatly depressing.)

If you don't give much or any money to a church or a charity, I understand the complexity of the issue. Rent, groceries, cars, college tuition, and nearly everything else makes us feel financially behind on a constant basis. But I do want to pass on this word from God's Word: **"A generous person will prosper; whoever refreshes others will be refreshed"** (Proverbs 11:25). While it is exciting to think about what riches can give you, God wants you to open your eyes to how generosity can bless you.

In this culture, you may find fewer and fewer examples of financial generosity. Perhaps our calling in this darkening world is to be bright lights of contentment, giving, and spiritual prosperity, rare people who can refresh others with open hands and open hearts.

Pray today for a financial reformation in America, and become a reformer who rejoices with every gift!

September 29

The greatest treasure
Ann Jahns

William Randolph Hearst Sr. was a wealthy American politician and newspaper magnate. One of his passions was amassing an extensive collection of international art. The story has been told that Hearst, in learning of a particularly enticing piece of art, sent one of his employees abroad to hunt down the treasure. It was eventually found—hidden away in Hearst's own warehouse, unseen. Hearst had amassed so many art treasures that he didn't realize he already owned it.

We might shake our heads at this story, but let's admit that we can relate to it. Few of us have the means to hunt down priceless art, but what earthly treasures do we seek obsessively? Money? Or stuff? Or notoriety? Or pleasure?

Jesus knows us. He knows our tendency to fill the empty spaces in our hearts with the things of this world—the empty spaces that only he can fill. He knows that our sinful hearts will always crave the treasures of this world. That's why he warns: **"Do not store up for yourselves treasures on earth, where moths and vermin destroy, and where thieves break in and steal. But store up for yourselves treasures in heaven, where moths and vermin do not destroy, and where thieves do not break in and steal. For where your treasure is, there your heart will be also"** (Matthew 6:19-21).

How human it is to be blind to the treasure that we already possess. Our salvation—the world's greatest treasure—is already ours through Jesus' life, death, and resurrection. We are rich indeed!

September 30

New mercies every morning
Nathan Nass

How often does the sun come up? Every morning. Some days it's cloudy. Some days it's raining. Some winter days the sun comes up late. But how often does the sun come up? Every single morning.

God wants us to take note of that, because that's how faithful he is. Actually, that's how faithful God's mercy and compassion are. In one of the lowest points of the Old Testament, in the middle of a heartbreaking book of lamentations for God's judgment on the sinful people of Jerusalem, it says: **"Because of the Lord's great love we are not consumed, for his compassions never fail. They are new every morning; great is your faithfulness"** (Lamentations 3:22,23). God gives new mercies every morning.

If we ever show mercy to other people, it's always a limited amount. Our mercy quickly ends, but not God's. As faithfully as the sun rises, God's mercies are new every morning. Whatever sins you committed yesterday are washed with Jesus' blood. Whatever guilt you've carried for months or years has been forgiven at Jesus' cross. As surely as the sun rises, God's mercies are new every morning.

That means there's hope for you today. There's hope today in Jesus! Even if your city is destroyed, like it was for the people of Jerusalem, even if your strength is gone, even if everyone else has run out of patience with you, God hasn't. When you see the sun rise, remember: There are new mercies every morning.

About the Writers

Pastor Mike Novotny pours his Jesus-based joy into his ministry as a pastor at The CORE (Appleton, Wisconsin) and as the lead speaker for Time of Grace, a global media ministry that points people to Jesus through television, print, and digital resources. Unafraid to bring grace and truth to the toughest topics of our time, he has written numerous books, including *3 Words That Will Change Your Life*, *When Life Hurts*, and *Taboo: Topics Christians Should Be Talking About but Don't*. Mike lives with his wife, Kim, and their two daughters, Brooklyn and Maya; runs long distances; and plays soccer with other middle-aged men whose best days are long behind them. To find more books by Pastor Mike, go to timeofgrace.store.

Linda Buxa is a freelance communications professional as well as a regular blogger and contributing writer for Time of Grace. Linda is the author of *Dig In! Family Devotions to Feed Your Faith*, *Parenting by Prayer*, *Made for Friendship*, *Visible Faith*, and *How to Fight Anxiety With Joy*. She and her husband, Greg, have lived in Alaska, Washington D.C., and California. After Greg retired from the military, they moved to Wisconsin, where they settled on 11.7 acres. Because their three children insisted on getting older, using their gifts, and pursuing goals, Greg and Linda recently entered the empty-nest stage of life. The sign in her kitchen sums up the past 24 years of marriage: "You call it chaos; we call it family."

Pastor Jon Enter served in West Palm Beach, Florida, for ten years. He is now a campus pastor and instructor at St. Croix Lutheran Academy in St. Paul, Minnesota. Jon also serves as a regular speaker and a contributing writer to

Time of Grace. He once led a tour at his college, and the Lord had him meet his future wife, Debbi. They have four daughters: Violet, Lydia, Eden, and Maggie.

Pastor Matt Ewart was born and raised in Oklahoma and has lived in several different places since then, including Nebraska, Utah, Wisconsin, Colorado, and Alaska (for a summer). He has served as a pastor at NorthCross Lutheran Church in Lakeville, Minnesota, since 2014. Before that he served churches located in Commerce City, Colorado, and Tempe, Arizona. Pastor Matt enjoys being outside, listening to podcasts, and tinkering with things in his free time.

Jan Gompper spent most of her career teaching theatre at Wisconsin Lutheran College in Milwaukee. She also served six years as a cohost for *Time of Grace* during its start-up years. She has collaborated on two faith-based musicals, numerous Christian songs, and has written and codirected scripts for a Christian video series. She and her husband now reside in the Tampa area, where she continues to practice her acting craft and coach aspiring acting students as opportunities arise. She also assists with Sunday school and other church-related activities.

Ann Jahns and her husband live in Wisconsin as empty nesters, having had the joy of raising three boys to adulthood. She is a marketing coordinator for a Christian church body and a freelance proofreader and copy editor. Ann has been privileged to teach Sunday school and lead Bible studies for women of all ages. One of her passions is supporting women in the "sandwich generation" as they experience the unique joys and challenges of raising children while supporting aging parents.

Pastor Daron Lindemann loves the journey—exploring God's paths in life with his wife or discovering even more about Jesus and the Bible. He serves as a pastor in Pflugerville, Texas, with a passion for life-changing faith and for smoking brisket.

Pastor Nathan Nass serves at Christ the King Lutheran Church in Tulsa, Oklahoma. Prior to moving to Oklahoma, he served at churches in Wisconsin, Minnesota, Texas, and Georgia. He and his wife, Emily, have five children. You can find more sermons and devotions on his blog: upsidedownsavior.home.blog.

Jason Nelson had a career as a teacher, counselor, and leader. He has a bachelor's degree in education, did graduate work in theology, and has a master's degree in counseling psychology. After his career ended in disabling back pain, he wrote the book *Miserable Joy: Chronic Pain in My Christian Life*. He has written and spoken extensively on a variety of topics related to the Christian life. Jason has been a contributing writer for Time of Grace since 2010. He has authored many Grace Moments devotions and several books. Jason lives with his wife, Nancy, in Wisconsin.

Pastor Dave Scharf served as a pastor in Greenville, Wisconsin, and now serves as a professor of theology at Martin Luther College in Minnesota. He has presented at numerous leadership, outreach, and missionary conferences across the country. He is a contributing writer and speaker for Time of Grace. Dave and his wife have six children.

Liz Schroeder is a Resilient Recovery coach, which is a ministry that allows her to go into sober living homes and share the love and hope of Jesus with men and women recently out of rehab or prison. It has been a dream of hers to write Grace Moments, a resource she has used for years in homeschooling her five children. After going on a mission trip to Malawi through an organization called Kingdom Workers, she now serves on its U.S. board of directors. She and her husband, John, are privileged to live in Phoenix and call CrossWalk their church home.

Matt Trotter is the president and CEO of Time of Grace Ministry. His responsibilities include ensuring the ministry stays true to its vision/mission, overseeing the business aspects of the ministry, shaping the strategic direction, and creating a culture in the organization that makes it the "best job ever" for every employee. Matt and his wife, MJ, have been blessed with five daughters of resplendent beauty and boundless energy. Together the family enjoys school, volleyball, swimming, and training their faithful dog, Mars.

C.L. Whiteside is a sports coach, educator, and podcaster. He has been blessed to work and be involved with people from all different walks of life, meeting some amazing people who have helped teach, guide, and provide him with unique insights. C.L. is married to Nicole and has a young daughter. Listen to C.L.'s podcast, *The Non-Microwaved Truth*, at timeofgrace.org or on Spotify, Apple Podcasts, or wherever you get your favorite podcasts.

Pastor Nate Wordell is a happy son of the King of the universe. He's absolutely smitten with his wife, Rachel, and he's doing his best to raise two little boys. He's a pastor at Wisconsin Lutheran College and was previously at Mount Olive Lutheran Church in Appleton, Wisconsin, and at Martin Luther College in New Ulm, Minnesota.

About Time of Grace

The mission of Time of Grace is to point people to what matters most: Jesus. Using a variety of media (television, radio, podcasts, print publications, and digital), Time of Grace teaches tough topics in an approachable and relatable way, accessible in multiple languages, making the Bible clear and understandable for those who need encouragement in their walks of faith and for those who don't yet know Jesus at all.

To discover more, please visit timeofgrace.org or scan this code:

Help share God's message of grace!

Every gift you give helps Time of Grace reach people around the world with the good news of Jesus. Your generosity and prayer support take the gospel of grace to others through our ministry outreach and help them experience a satisfied life as they see God all around them.

Give today at timeofgrace.org/give, by calling 800.661.3311, or by scanning the code below.

Thank you!

TIME OF GRACE®